STO

ALLEN COUNTY PUBLIC LIBRARY

FRIENDS
OF AC

P9-DBJ-568

THE
WILD
ONE

Also by ETH CLIFFORD

Burning Star
Search for the Crescent Moon
The Year of the Three-Legged Deer

Eth Clifford

THE
WILD
ONE

Illustrated by Arvis Stewart

Houghton Mifflin Company Boston 1974

Library of Congress Cataloging in Publication Data

Clifford, Eth, 1915–
    The wild one.

    SUMMARY: A fictionalized biography stressing the turbulent
boyhood of the man who "hating" medicine in his youth went on
to become a renowned scientist winning the Nobel Prize for
medicine in 1906.
    1. Ramón y Cajal, Santiago, 1852–1934—Juvenile fiction. [1.
Ramón y Cajal, Santiago, 1852–1934—Fiction. 2. Physicians,
Spanish—Fiction] I. Stewart, Arvis L., illus. II. Title.
PZ7.C62214Wi [Fic]   74-8899
ISBN 0-395-19491-1

COPYRIGHT (C) 1974 BY ETHEL CLIFFORD ROSENBERG
ALL RIGHTS RESERVED. NO PART OF THIS WORK MAY BE
REPRODUCED OR TRANSMITTED IN ANY FORM BY ANY MEANS,
ELECTRONIC OR MECHANICAL, INCLUDING PHOTOCOPYING AND
RECORDING, OR BY ANY INFORMATION STORAGE OR RETRIEVAL
SYSTEM, WITHOUT PERMISSION IN WRITING FROM THE PUBLISHER.
PRINTED IN THE UNITED STATES OF AMERICA
FIRST PRINTING A

This book is dedicated
to the memory of my brother
Maurice Clifford
who knew what it was to be
the wild one

2076938

THE
WILD
ONE

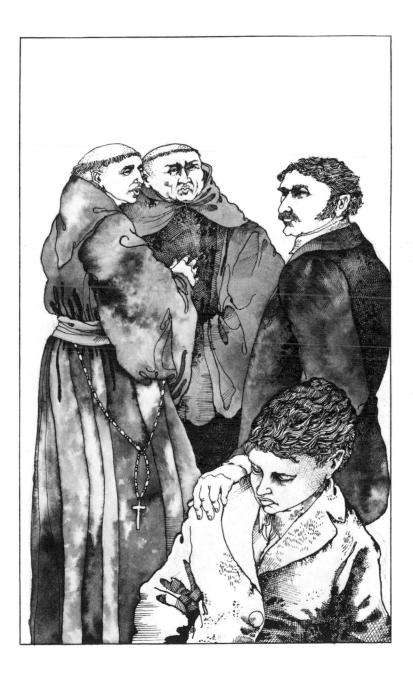

Foreword

IT IS AN OLD TRUISM that "truth is stranger than fiction." Perhaps nowhere can this truism be better applied than to the life of Santiago Ramón y Cajal, one of the foremost scientists of his time. He was born May 1, 1852, in Petilla de Aragón, a small town of Navarre in Spain, a hamlet so remote and inaccessible that, when he revisited it as an adult, he could reach it only by mule and with the help of a guide.

His growing years were characterized by rebellion, mischief, and a determination to resist all schooling. So backward was he in his studies that his father, who had great ambition for his son to follow in his own footsteps as a doctor, at last, in despair, apprenticed the boy to a barber and subsequently to two cobblers. In today's language, the young Santiago would have been considered an almost incorrigible juvenile delinquent.

Ramón y Cajal did finally catch fire from his studies. A pioneer in neuroanatomy, he devoted himself to the study of histology, a branch of anatomy having to do with the microscopic structure of tissues.

In 1879, he became the director of the medical museum of the Zaragoza University; in 1883, professor of descriptive anatomy in Valencia; in 1887, professor of histology and pathological anatomy in Barcelona. From 1892 to 1922, when he retired at the age of seventy, he held the chair of histology and pathological anatomy at the University of Madrid.

The young boy who "hated" medicine was destined to become a world figure recognized and honored for his research in neuroanatomy. It was Santiago Ramón y Cajal who was responsible for the establishment of the neuron, or nerve cell, as the basic unit of the nervous system. At a time when little was known about the cerebellum and the cerebrum, he researched the field and published a massive amount of material in a veritable flood of scientific monographs. In 1906, Santiago Ramón y Cajal was awarded the Nobel Prize for medicine for his work on the structure of the nervous system. He received titles, decorations, prizes, and honorary degrees not only in his native Spain but from countries around the world, including the United States, a list so long it would take several pages to enumerate them.

In addition to his scientific works, he wrote a number of books, including, shortly before his death on October 17, 1934, at the age of eighty-two, a book entitled *El Mundo Visto a los Ochenta Años* (*The World as Seen at Eighty*). He also wrote his autobiography, *Recuerdas de mi vida* (*Recollections of My Life*), which was published in Madrid in 1901, and which was first published in English as Volume 8 of Memoirs of the

American Philosophical Society of Philadelphia, Pennsylvania. The author wishes to acknowledge with grateful thanks the use of the American Philosophical Society's edition of *Recollections of My Life* which served as the primary source for *The Wild One*.

Although *The Wild One* deals with a real man and the turbulence of his growing years, it must be remembered that this is a work of fiction. To carry the story forward, the thoughts, dialogue, and some of the characters are necessarily fictional as well. Almost all the incidents related in this book did occur, but they do not adhere strictly to the time sequence in which they actually happened.

A number of fine adult books have been written about Santiago Ramón y Cajal dealing with the whole man from infancy to death but primarily focused on Ramón y Cajal the scientist. In *The Wild One*, I concentrated on the growing boy, for the rebellion, the dreams, the frustrations and the sensitivities of youth span the ages and are timeless.

ONE

My FATHER HATES ME, his oldest-born son. I do not say this because he beats me. He whips my brother Pedro also. We do some piece of mischief and we are punished. This I accept. No, it is not so small a thing, though the beatings make my body ache for days, that tells me how he feels. It is the coldness in his eyes. When a man scourges a boy, something should come alive in his face — anger, passion, fury. My father passes sentence and carries it out, and no emotion touches him.

My mother defends him. This is natural. My mother is a loving woman. You have only to look at her to know this. In the church, there is a painting of the Madonna. I do not know if the painting is a good one or not, but often I go to church for no other reason than to stare at the Madonna, the sad one, with the large, brown, elongated eyes which speak of the sorrows of the world, the long, beautiful nose, the tender lips. So my mother looks to me.

Father Miguel stares at me suspiciously whenever he catches me staring at the painting. Always he says the same thing in his dusty dry voice. "Have you come to repent your sins, Santiago?"

I suppose in the eyes of God and the priests I am a sinner. I do not have to wonder how I appear to the people of my village. To them, I am the wild one. Let something happen in the village and they do not have to seek far to find the guilty one. Who else would think of such a thing? Not *their* sons! So, if I am to blame or not, the finger points to me, Santiago Ramón y Cajal.

Did my father love me once? I do not remember, but I think it may be so, for when I was little, very little, he took much time with me. I am fourteen now, but it still remains clear in my mind how, when I was four or so, he held me by the hand and we walked from the village. He was like a giant to me then, this tall, stern-looking man with the bright black eyes, the swarthy, clean-shaven face and the strong, large hands. Good hands, I suppose, for a surgeon.

How surprised I was, I recall, when we stopped at last before an abandoned shepherd's cave. I was afraid. I did not want to leave the brilliance of our Spanish sun for the darkness of that forbidding cave, but my father urged me on.

"Do you know why I have brought you here?" my father asked.

I glanced anxiously about, trying to penetrate the blackness of the corridors that fled from the outer chamber into the heart of the mountainside, fearful of some dread monster or supernatural being waiting to leap out at us. I shook my head. "No, Papa."

"Your mother thinks you are a baby, Santiago. Are you a baby?"

"No, Papa," I replied obediently. "Pedro is the baby." Pedro is two years younger than I.

"You are four years old, Santiago. Soon you will be a man. There are many things you must learn. The lessons must begin now — today."

"Papa?" I questioned him timidly. "Why can we not begin the lessons at home?"

"There are too many interruptions. People come for me to treat them. Your good mother hovers. Here we can be alone. We will begin with French."

My eyes filled with tears. I did not wish to learn to speak French. Was not my own native Spanish sufficiently difficult, since my father corrected me constantly, saying I was not to speak the patois of the streets but the language of the poets?

How I came to dread those daily pilgrimages to the cave. I learned — my father was too good a teacher to fail in his objective — but I think it was then I first fell into the habit of mischief.

One day I hid when it was time to go to the cave. I secreted myself in the barn of a neighbor, peeping through a crack in the loft, laughing to myself softly as I heard first my father and then my mother calling my name, my mother with some anxiety, my father with growing impatience. I did not come out and so, after a while, they gave up. I jumped down then and turned my attention to *El Viejo*, the old one, the horse that pulled back its ugly mouth and showed its teeth when anyone approached him. He was mean, that one,

3

bad-tempered, a difficult animal, as lean and dried-up as the people of our village. A man from Barcelona passed through our village once. I heard him tell my father that our people are as harsh and unyielding as the land we live on, our Aragonese tablelands that sit in the shadow of the Pyrenees mountains, burning under our implacable sun.

"Do not show your teeth to me," I said with some bravura, approaching him slowly. "You have been free long enough. Now it is time for me to teach you things you should know." *El Viejo* watched me, snorting. I should have been warned that he was not in the best of moods when he began to paw the ground and toss his head wildly. But I was too intent upon my new game.

. "You will learn," I repeated. Had I not learned to read and write, to add sums, to puzzle over geography? Then this wretched animal could also learn to obey commands, to do tricks, to respond to my voice. I would be a teacher like my father, the great Don Justo Ramón Casasús. Perhaps *El Viejo* felt about learning as I did, for when I approached too closely, he lashed out at me wildly, his forelegs boxing the air. He screamed, too, I remember, a high, piercing whinny that brought his owner to the barn on the run in time to find me unconscious on the floor, my forehead bleeding profusely.

My father cared for me, allowing no one to touch me. He was at my side day and night; this my mother has often told me. Yet when I was completely recovered, what was my father's first act? He required

4

me to bring him the whip, and thus I received my first beating at his hands. Was it then my father ceased to love me?

He will beat me again tonight, as soon as he finds out what happened today. But I will not stay. As soon as the fiesta is over tomorrow, I will run away. I have run away before, but this time — I swear it — I will not come back.

As regards this afternoon, let me tell you what happened. We were in school; Father Miguel was droning on as usual. I was drawing in my catechism — that is a mortal sin and I know it. But there is something in me which cannot resist a blank space. My fingers itch for a pencil, a paint brush. And the columns of print in the catechism are surrounded by such beautiful white areas! So there I was, head bent over my work, when of a sudden Father Miguel fetched me a clout that made my head swim and my ears ring.

"Sacrilege!" Father Miguel sputtered. "The work of the Evil One. Don Justo shall hear of this day's mischief."

"Please, Padre," my brother Pedro begged. "Do not tell Papa. He will beat Santiago again."

"Shall he be spared a beating and endanger his immortal soul?" Father Miguel snapped. "No. The good doctor shall certainly be told." He picked up the catechism and held it under my nose, his hands shaking with rage. "Sacrilege!" he cried again. He made me sit on a high stool in the corner of the room. I did not mind, for now I was able to stare out the window. There is not usually much to see; only the courtyard and the bell tower and the sky beyond. As I looked, I saw Father Félipe step briskly across the court. He paused and frowned up at the sky, then held his head tilted to one side, listening. I heard it then, too, the sound of thunder. Storms come up quickly in our part of the country. One moment the sky is implacably blue, the next moment the sun disappears behind black clouds that rise above the mountains, shrouding the peaks and obscuring the ruins of the ancient feudal castle perched on top of one of the pinnacles.

The thunder grew louder, roaring through the narrow, stepped streets of our village, which huddles at the foot of the mountain. Lightning forked from the sky, seeking out objects below in a random pattern. Father Félipe ran across the courtyard, his black cassock billowing in the fast-growing wind; it gave him the appearance of flying along the ground. He vanished inside the bell tower and I could not see him, but I knew he was climbing the steps.

Father Félipe is a man much bound by duty. Whenever we have a storm, he climbs the tower to ring the large, greening bronze bell to warn us, as if we are incapable of looking up at the sky ourselves! Even as he was mounting the steps, the rain fell in hard, driving gusts. Inside the classroom, the students paid no attention to the storm, for Father Miguel never permitted a lesson to be interrupted. I stared out the window again. Father Félipe was just emerging at the top of the tower. I could see him visibly steeling himself to face the knife-edge sharpness of the wind. Then he stepped out into the tower, reached for the bell ropes and began the hard, downward pull.

I have never seen a man die before; it is a sight to chill the soul. Lightning leaped from the sky. Like the finger of God, it pierced Father Félipe, lifting him from his feet and flinging him across the railing, where he lay limp and uncaring, his dead eyes staring sightless into the rain. I rose from my seat, shouting "Father Félipe!"

Father Miguel wheeled about, his face purpling with anger. He is a small man; perhaps that is why his rage mounts to his head so quickly. "Do you disrupt my class again, Santiago?"

"Father Félipe is dead," I whispered.

"Wicked boy!" Father Miguel was shocked. "Do you dare tell me such a lie in this room? Do you not hear the bell tolling? Who else but Father Félipe pulls the ropes? You will remain when the others leave, do you understand? Now back to the corner and not another word. Not another word."

He turned from me and glared at the other students, who were grinning at me and whispering to one another.

"What?" Father Miguel shouted. "By whose leave have you ceased your prayers? We will resume." Together they began intoning where they had left off. "Lord, deliver us from all evil . . ."

Suddenly our small building shuddered. As blood flows after the knife that sheds it, so our schoolhouse yielded to the bolt of lightning which struck it, entering capriciously through an open window just above our room, shattering our ceiling, and raining down upon us debris and fragments of plaster before disappearing down through a hole in the far end of the wooden floor. In moments we were covered with choking, white dust that blinded our eyes and burned our throats. A strong, sulfurous odor pervaded the air. In panic, the students began to mill about, so beset with fear that they forgot where the door was.

I sat frozen in my corner, staring straight ahead to where a statue of Mother Mary with the child Jesus in her arms swung crazily upon a nail, then fell and crashed, disintegrating into powder and shards on the floor. To see a priest die and a holy relic destroyed is a mind-shattering experience. If my brother Pedro had not rushed to my side and propelled me from the room, I do not think I would have moved from that spot.

"We will choke to death in this place," he screamed in my ear. He tugged at my sleeve until I followed him obediently.

Outside, the storm was already passing, departing with a few last grumblings overhead. In a matter of moments, the sun began to heat the day; the sky was soon a brilliant blue again, almost innocent of clouds. Some mothers had gathered in the courtyard, waiting anxiously for their children to emerge. Now, as we came stumbling out of the doorway, our faces and clothing white with plaster dust, some bleeding from cuts on faces and arms, a woman shrieked. "*Madre de Dios!*" Like a goat separating her kid from the flock, she pounced upon Hernando, one of the smaller boys in our class. She herded him to her vast bosom with little comforting cries, wiping his tears away with the corner of her apron. Thus, one by one were first the littler ones and then the older boys claimed. Our mother was not there; never would my father permit her to rush through the streets. Not so should the wife of the distinguished *médico* comport herself.

In the turmoil, I had forgotten Father Félipe. Now I looked up. His body was still there, slumped over the railing. "Pedro, look there," I pointed.

If one looks upward, then two, then all in a crowd will put back their heads and stare upward likewise. Mothers and children, following the direction of my pointing finger, were instantly shocked into silence. They stood open-mouthed, staring at the dead priest in the bell tower. Even as we watched, Father Félipe's body slid down from the railing and slumped on the floor near the bell, which had long ceased its tolling. The women fell to their knees, some crossing themselves and muttering quick prayers, others clutching at large silver crosses hung round their necks.

Behind me, I heard a sound. It was Father Miguel. His eyes burned as he stared. Then he said hollowly, "It is a judgment! A judgment," he repeated. His fingers dug into my arm.

I do not care if he is a priest. He is a cruel man. If it is a sin to say this, then I will take this sin upon my soul. Father Félipe was not cruel. He was not my friend — what adult in my village is? — but he did not seek to triumph over me in small matters as Father Miguel does. He is full of the righteousness that

9

destroys the will of others, as soft water erodes hard rock, drop by drop.

I tried to free my arm, but Father Miguel dug his fingers deeper. At last I could bear it no more and struck his arm, a swift, downward blow that loosened his grip.

Hernando's mother gasped. "He struck Father Miguel. I saw it with my own eyes. That wicked Santiago struck a priest."

I turned and started to run from the courtyard.

"Catch him," another woman said. "Why do you let him go?" she demanded.

Father Miguel sighed. "Where can he go?" he replied. "Can the sinner flee from his sins?"

This much I heard before I fled, knowing that Father Miguel would lose no time in presenting himself to my father. And my father will listen, of course, his lips compressed. Then when Father Miguel leaves, my father will reproach my mother for her softness, and when I come home, *if* I come home, he will beat me, first with the whip and then with the cudgel.

But no matter what happens, I will not miss the fiesta. That I have promised myself. I will not miss the fiesta.

TWO

I WILL TELL YOU something you may not believe. I am fourteen, and my mind and my body are a battlefield. Is such a thing comprehensible to you? I wish I could see matters so clearly as my father sees them. He has no doubts, no inner turmoils. Often have I heard, from his lips, from my mother, from my uncles, the story of his life: how he, as the youngest son of a farmer, had no claim to the meager portion of land his father bequeathed to the older brothers and consequently was forced to go out in the world to make his living. He apprenticed himself to a surgeon and there, in Javierre de Latre, a village even smaller than our own, my father dwelt for ten years, becoming both barber and blood-letter under the careful scrutiny of his master. For another, perhaps, such an existence would have been enough, but my father was an ambitious man. Having studied all the books in his master's library, my father conceived a daring plan; he determined to go to Barcelona to study medicine. He walked every step of the way from Javierre de Latre to Barcelona, from the banks of the Gállego River to the shores of the Mediterranean Sea, some 300 miles, a distance to stagger the mind! There he once again worked as a barber and meanwhile attended also the university, and after much travail and deprivation, emerged as a surgeon, highest in his class.

Who can live up to such perfection? When I have protested, saying I cannot grasp this or the other, my father dismisses such objections as trivial. What? Too young at four to deal with French and arithmetic and geography? Six years of age, and baffled by Greek? Nonsense. Am I not the son of my father? Has not the good Lord given me a mind? Life upon this earth is short, too short for man to learn all that he can, all that he should; therefore, he must not waste a moment. An infant learns from birth on. My father warms to a subject dearest to his heart. But I am not my father. I am myself, Santiago Ramón y Cajal. And what is this self that is called by this name? I do not know! I feel sometimes that there struggle within me many different Santiagoes — the Santiago who dreams, who wanders adrift, alone, seeking the solitude of the woods and the river flowing restless to the sea; the Santiago who is seized with so overwhelming an urge to draw that he must paint or die! And then there is the other Santiago, that Santiago the villagers call the wild one, who leads the boys into acts of witless vandalism and violence; Santiago, the rebel, whose body is flagellated by the whip and the cudgel, who weeps and despairs and sins again.

After I had run from Father Miguel, I started to race for the woods to brood, but then I changed my mind. I went instead to the public square to seek out Francisco and Juan, Lope, José, and Claudio. These are my friends now, especially Lope, though they had been my enemies once. They had made fun of me, mocking me, calling me, in their curious Aragonese tongue, *forano*, the foreigner. And all because I was not, like the children of the village, clothed in breeches and sandals, and did not wear the prescribed handkerchief bound securely about my head! This was in the beginning, when we had first moved to the village.

Do you know anything of Ayerbe, the town in which I live? It sits on the road from Huesca to Jaca, looking up at the mountains. Ayerbe is not big, as Barcelona is big, or even Zaragoza, but we are not so small that we do not have our public square, which is really not one but two squares in the heart of the town. In the center, separating the two squares, is the palace in which the marquis and his family live when they are in residence. In the lower square, adjoining the palace, is our beautiful clock tower. Here are the fiestas held, and many fairs. Our fairs are well known. Merchants from other villages flock to Ayerbe on fair days. In the other square, I meet with my friends and we plot what we shall do next.

When I arrived, Francisco, Juan, and Claudio were spinning tops; Lope and José were pushing one another around out of sheer boredom.

"Hey, Santiago! *Qué pasa?*" Lope yelled joyfully. The others gathered up their tops and ran toward me.

"Santiago is here. Now we can go to the threshing floor and have a stone fight," José asserted.

José has not too much imagination, you understand. I made for him, and for the others, of course, slings. José's I constructed of goatskin, which he took from his father's shop without permission. For Lope, Juan, Francisco, and Claudio I had to make use of leather from our boots. Our boots suffered, and our bottoms did likewise, for all our fathers fell upon us with equal rage for the mutilation of good, sturdy footwear, but I can tell you no one else in Ayerbe had such slings. Since then, José has become most proficient in the use of the sling. He has even hunted game; partridges are his favorite, but he is good even with the fleet rabbits which forage in the orchards. And all he wishes is to use the sling. As I say, not one who has much imagination.

"No," I told him. "We will not go to the threshing floor." I pointed up, to the mountain peak. We will go to the castle and wage war."

"And you will tell us stories?" Francisco said slyly, grinning.

"And if the mood suits me, I will tell you marvelous tales," I replied grandly.

I do not deny it. I have the advantage. These friends of mine are sons of the farmers hereabouts. Their fathers, unlike my own, do not concern themselves with such things as education. Can the sons read and write passably? Do they study their catechism? Enough. So their language is slipshod, not the pure Castilian my father insists we speak at home, but the patois of the street, that dialogue which is a mongrel mixture of Castilian and Catalan and Aragonese and who knows what else. What more does a man need to wrest a living from the stubborn, arid soil? Will the earth flourish, plants thrive, rain fall if he can conjugate a verb in French or read a passage from Plato in Greek?

So they reason, and the sons are little disposed to argue. Yet they enjoy my stories nevertheless. And I? Where and when had I come to know the tales I spin? My father does not approve of works of fiction. Frivolity, he says, frowning. My mother, the romantic one, had some books hidden in a trunk. She had read them before her marriage to my father but had not looked at them since, for she would not willingly disobey her husband. I had heard her mention them once, so, seeking them out, I removed them one by one secretly to my room. There I read them aloud to my brother Pedro, who listened nervously, one eye always upon the door lest our father come in and discover us. Cheap, romantic trash, my father calls it, but no book shall ever be so exquisite an experience to me again as the one called *The Count of Monte Cristo*.

I never tired of reading or telling this and other stories so long as I had an eager audience. But I changed my mind when my brother Pedro came running across the square to join us.

"Do you know what I have heard?" he gasped. "Tomorrow night at the fiesta. Do you know who will be there? The general himself! What do you say to that?"

The boys crowded around Pedro.

"Where did you hear this?"

"Who tells you this?"

"General Prim is coming *here*, to our village? I do not believe you," Lope said, yet his voice held much hope.

I laughed. Pedro's face grew red. He does not like me to make fun of him, but sometimes I must. He is such an innocent, that one, so good, so trusting. Pedro will believe almost anything you tell him. I think it is because he is like my mother, loving. Me, I am like my father in one way, that is sure. I am cold and logical.

"Why would someone of such importance in our country come to some little fiesta in a village no one has ever heard of?" I asked.

"We are not so unimportant as all that," Claudio said resentfully. "Perhaps the general comes to visit the marquis, or do you not consider the palace of the marquis grand enough for so important a man?"

"Would you come to Ayerbe if you could go anywhere in Spain, to Barcelona, or Granada, or Madrid? Would you eat with a marquis if you could dine with a king, or a queen?" I demanded.

"Oh, let us get on with it," Francisco said impatiently. "Are we going to the ruins, or are we going to stand here gossiping like the old ones?" He bent his body and began to hobble about, calling in a falsetto, "*Buenos días*, Señora Madera. Is it true what I hear, that your husband will not confess even to the padre what took place when he went to Jaca? No need to deny it, Señora. Ah, Señora Valdez, I was just saying to Señora Madera, if two know a secret, it is a secret no longer. Is it true what they are whispering about your oldest daughter, Consuela?"

We had to laugh, even Pedro, for Francisco is a devil of a fellow when he imitates María Ruíz, an old witch of a woman who lives alone at the edge of the town with no family except a mangy donkey who is as stubborn as she is, and possibly almost as curious.

"No," I decided. "Let us forget about the ruins." I watched their faces fall. When we go to the ancient castle high on the peak, we play old war games. Many a cuirass and helmet I have made for them. It is truly wonderful what one can do with bits of cardboard and old tins and lots of imagination. Arrows, too, I have constructed, good, true arrows, with smooth, straight shafts whittled from bamboo. I do not use nails, as the others do, for arrowheads, but broken awls which the shoemaker discards. As for the bows, green boxwood is excellent for it lends itself to being bent, is strong and quite elastic.

"Shall we steal some fruit, then?" Juan suggested. Raiding orchards is an old pastime with us. This my father has never understood. "Do we not have plentiful fruit in our own orchard that you must go and steal from our neighbors? Does not our table groan with the fruit my patients bring?" And he beats me until I cannot stand it and I shout, "All right! All right! I promise!" But some evil spirit drives me, and when the others head for the orchards, I go with them. Why? Why do I do these things?

"I have a better idea," I said.

They crowded around me. They know from the

18

look on my face when I have begun some fertile plan.

"Let us construct a cannon."

They stared at me in awe. Construct a cannon? One that shoots? How was it possible?

"Listen," I said. "To begin with, we will need some tools and materials. In our barn, we have a piece of beam. You know where it is, Pedro?" Pedro nodded. It was an old beam left over from some construction work my father had ordered done in our home. "Lope, your father has an auger and sandpaper. Perhaps he would be so gracious as to lend you these things?" Lope's father is a carpenter. "Of course," Lope said, grinning at me. "Is not my father a gracious man?"

"Francisco, can you obtain wire and tarred cord?"

It is unnecessary to question Francisco regarding such things. Where and how Francisco acquires our supplies from time to time he does not say, nor do I press him. Am I not always in sufficient trouble without knowing this as well? Francisco is such a one that if you were to say to him, "Francisco, I desire the breath of a goat and the dream of a hare," he would nod quietly, melt away, and return with the objects requested.

"We will meet in the orchard behind my house," I shouted after Francisco as he left our circle.

Everyone left quickly to pick up the needed materials. When we came together again in my father's orchard, I began carefully to bore a hole in the center of the beam. Lope objected at first, saying angrily that, since it was his father's auger I was using, he

19

should work on the beam, but the others shouted him down. What did Lope know of making a cannon, they argued furiously. For that matter, I thought, what did I know, but because they were aware of my superior though reluctantly acquired education, the task remained mine. After I got the hole started, we took turns boring with the auger, for it was hot in the sun and the work somewhat tedious.

"There! It's —nished," Jose said enthusiastically, when the boring of the beam was done at last.

"Finished? Far from it. There is much yet to be done," I told him, but as it happened, we could not work further on the cannon for at that moment my mother called us away. "Bring sandpaper," I shouted to Lope as Pedro and I left. "And we will all meet here tomorrow to finish the cannon."

And so it was. Next morning we met as planned. I was still sore from the whipping my father had given me when I arrived home — Father Miguel had wasted no time in the telling of his tale — but I did not let this deter me from going ahead with the making of the cannon.

I picked up the beam and examined it carefully.

"Now," I said, squinting professionally down the opening, "we will have to smooth it out. Have you brought the sandpaper, Lope?"

"Of course I have brought the sandpaper. The question is, Santiago, how you will apply the sandpaper into such a long narrow space."

"Look for a long thick branch or twig," I instructed. They scattered and brought me a variety of twigs and branches which I scrutinized, at last picking one that Pedro had selected. He smiled happily at the others, proud that he was contributing as much as they. Carefully, I tied the sandpaper around my improvised ramrod; I worked it around and around inside the beam until I was satisfied I could get it no smoother.

"It will need to be reinforced so that when we put the powder in, the cannon will not fly apart," I announced with some authority.

"Exactly so," Lope agreed. "It needs to be reinforced."

"There is an old oil can in the barn," Pedro said dubiously. "Shall I fetch it?"

I nodded. The tin from the can would serve the purpose quite well.

When I had the tin carefully set in place, Lope pounded me on the back. "It is done," he shouted gleefully. "Now we must shoot it."

"Not so fast," I protested. "To begin with, we must mount it on wheels. Furthermore, I wish to save it for the fiesta tonight. What more appropriate, eh?"

I do not know if I have mentioned it, but the fiesta, of course, was being held to celebrate our exciting attack on the city of Tetuan in Morocco. Our generals, Prim and O'Donnell, had defeated Muley-el-Abbas. The Moors were falling to our brave Spanish soldiers in Africa. The splendor that was ours long ago would be ours again. The Spanish flag would unfurl in the breeze, triumphing over a foreign city. I burned with patriotic fervor, I who had never seen a Moor, and to whom Africa was but a blob on the map. But it was the temper of the times, and the good Lord knew there was little enough for us to celebrate in our harsh Aragón.

"But how will we know if the cannon really works?" Juan objected. "Surely it would be only sensible to try it out?"

"We have no choice but to try it," Claudio added sagely.

"Agreed. We try it," Lope said.

"On what?" Francisco asked. A good question. It was then I made a brilliant suggestion. At the moment, at any rate, it seemed to me an idea little short of inspired. I did not wish to see anyone come to harm; if the target were some inanimate object, whom could it hurt? Furthermore, in spite of my conception of how one builds a cannon, I was not so certain as I made it seem that it would work at all.

"Let us attack Señor Hidalgo's gate." Señor Hidalgo is our neighbor. The gate was a new one he had just installed, but if you will give the matter some serious consideration, you will understand why this gate was for me such a logical choice. Beyond Señor Hidalgo's gate there is only a long, narrow lane that is bordered on either side by high walls. It is an alley that is used at best by a stray dog or chicken, but is more frequently completely deserted. "We will mount the cannon on this wall," I said, patting the stone wall behind me. "It will be exactly the right height for aiming at the gate. But first we must prime the cannon."

To obtain gunpowder was no problem. My father is

a famed hunter, one who often is seen in pursuit of game, his gun resting lightly in his huge hands. The delicate task of loading the powder into the bore I allowed no one to do, but I permitted Lope to stuff it with a large wad, and each took his turn filling the bore with small stones. As to the fuse, this, too, I retained as my sole responsibility. I poured a generous amount of gunpowder into the priming hole, and carefully, very carefully, placed in position a rather large fuse which I had fashioned from touchwood, an easily ignitible substance. Naturally, we had first lifted the cannon to an advantageous location upon the orchard wall, facing the gate. It was a moment of magnitude when I applied the match to the fuse. I shouted, "Run!" And run we did, our hearts pounding so that I could clearly see the pulse throbbing in Juan's throat.

Perhaps the explosion was not so loud as it appeared to us, but I would not have been surprised if its reverberations did not echo clear to Zaragoza. We danced around one another, clapping each other's backs in high good humor, shouting, "*Magnífico! Espléndido!*" Then we went to inspect the gate, or, that is to say, what was left of it. The gate still hung on its hinges, but the center was a mass of splintered wood. Over the gate there now appeared a face contorted with rage.

"*Bandidos! Demonios!*" Señor Hidalgo's voice was hoarse with anguish. "Regard my new gate!" He began to hurl small rocks at us in a paroxysm of frenzy, meanwhile cursing us with much vigor for a man of his years. Naturally, we dispersed, scattering in every direction. I had decided that I would be whipped in any case; how much more could happen? Therefore Pedro and I went quickly to our room. But I did not expect the dire consequences which followed my foolhardy adventure, or that I would, because of what ensued, miss the fiesta after all.

THREE

THE MAYOR OF OUR VILLAGE is a morose man, gaunt of face, with humorless eyes. He regards with suspicion those who do not nod instant agreement with his pronouncements; the position of his office, he believes, renders him infallible in all things. He has much respect for my father; however, he is certain that my father's political views border upon treason. The mayor is a monarchist, a staunch supporter of Isabella the Second. My father, on the other hand, is a republican, who believes that it is inevitable that the monarchy is doomed. Rumors of rebellion have swept even our village, which is so far removed from the mainstream of life in Spain. Consequently, the mayor is polite. My father is equally courteous. The amenities are studiously observed, but the mayor avoids my father when possible, and as for my father — well, he is not one to suffer fools gladly.

I tell you this so you will understand that a visit from the mayor to our house is a matter of some portent. As it happened, my father was at the door when the mayor arrived.

"Señor Doctor," the mayor said. "I must speak with you on a subject of some gravity."

My father opened the door wider. "My house is your house," he responded politely.

The mayor entered, and bustling in behind him came the constable, who made up for his unease at being in the presence of my father by being overly hearty and effusive. "*Buenas noches*, Señor Doctor. How goes it with your family? Your good wife is well, I trust . . ."

"Do not babble," the mayor interrupted him abruptly. "This is not a social visit."

My father raised his eyebrows.

"To what, then, do I owe the honor of your presence in my home, Mayor Pavía?"

"I have come to arrest your son Santiago and put him in jail."

My father's face darkened. Pedro and I had stolen part way down the steps when we had heard the mayor at the door. Now Pedro gasped, softly, but my father has keen ears. He turned and motioned us downward with but a single, hard glance. Mayor Pavía and the constable waited silently while we descended.

"What is the charge?" asked my father. While the mayor outlined the latest grievance against me — Señor Hidalgo's complaint had been accompanied by the irrefutable proof of the splintered gate — my father listened grimly. "And so, with your kind permission," Mayor Pavía concluded, somewhat maliciously, for he has long regarded me as a threat to the peace of our village, "the constable will now escort him to the *cárcel*."

"By all means," my father agreed.

The constable seemed somewhat dazed by my father's prompt acquiescence. Since it was obvious that my father would not lift a finger to save me, I felt I needed to offer some words in my defense.

"Señor," I pleaded with Mayor Pavía. "I cannot deny that it was my cannon that wrought such damage to Señor Hidalgo's gate, and for this I am sorry. But I did not believe the cannon would work. Truly I did not."

"Still it was a satisfactory blast, no doubt," the constable commented. I looked at him; his eyes were merry. He has four sons of his own; he is not entirely unacquainted with the mischief that boys are capable of when the days are long and time passes slowly.

At this moment, my mother burst in upon us. She had been listening at the door to the next room and could contain herself no longer.

"Santiago has done a terrible thing," she cried, her face flushed with excitement, "but surely we can come to some understanding. To put a young boy in confinement is a bad thing. Surely we can pay Señor Hidalgo for the gate . . ."

"Señora," Mayor Pavía interrupted. "I am not a hard man." He is not hard as granite is not hard; for this you have my word. "But this is not Santiago's first offense." He then began a recital of my supposed criminal activities, almost all of which had been perpetrated by others. I knew that it would be useless

27

to deny anything. My reputation is such that wrongdoing of any nature is easy to lay upon me. And I am aware that even my friends will allow me to be accused to escape punishment. I have long since learned to accept this. Unlike my father, I do not seek perfection in my fellow man.

"We will certainly pay for the gate," my father agreed. My mother smiled tremulously in great relief. "However," he continued, "Santiago shall go to jail and serve his sentence . . . for how long?" he inquired. "For four days," he agreed, when the mayor informed him how much time I would spend in the *cárcel*, "and I further suggest that it would do him great good to fast while he is there."

"No food?" my mother cried, aghast. "He will starve."

"Antonia, my angel. Have you not some duty in the kitchen that demands your attention?" my father said sternly. He turned to the constable. "Take your prisoner," he commanded. "And remember, I forbid you to feed him."

The mayor took polite leave; it was perhaps the first time that I saw a smile touch his lips. The constable, on the other hand, was much disturbed. "It is unnatural," he muttered under his breath. "Unnatural." He shook his head sadly but I knew that he would not disobey my father. Indeed, who would willingly cross Don Justo Ramón Casasús?

I must tell you that I do not take easily to confinement, as who does, for that matter? I cannot speak for others, but mine is a spirit that demands to be free. I am by nature, despite the fact that I do have a few friends, one who enjoys solitude and the comfort of my own thoughts. This is an aspect of their son my parents cannot conceive. Who would seek the solace of nature, the lonely contemplation of dusk quietly muting the river to a gentle rippling beneath the trees, or lie still in a ravine, absorbed by the activity of its restless inhabitants when he could be in the company of his peers? My father sees many people; my mother, though she is a gentle woman, cannot abide silence. For her the days must be filled with the sounds of life around her — voices, the clattering of pots and pans, the braying of the donkeys, the creaking of carts. Neither one understands the enchantment the springs, the hills, the very rocks hold for me. Often, in a veritable frenzy, I have tried to capture on paper these sights that sing in my heart. The drawings are well hidden in my room. My father would destroy them as frivolity.

Even as I walked side by side with the constable, his hand resting lightly upon my arm lest I attempt to escape, I could not believe that my sentence would be carried out. I tried reasoning with him.

"Señor," I implored. "I have a horror of being locked in."

He gave me a side glance. "So you should. A prison is no place for a man, only an animal."

My heart quickened. He, at least, understood. But he continued placidly, "Still, there are some who cannot learn and go constantly against authority. These are the ones who keep our jails full." He shook

29

his head. "We create our own problems and then we cry out about the unfairness of the world. Who, for example," he warmed to his subject, "insisted that you construct a cannon — a remarkable achievement for one so young," he added, but went on quickly lest I feel he approved, "and with it destroy Señor Hidalgo's gate, eh? Did you expect the world to applaud?" He glanced about quickly and dropped his voice. "I am the father of sons. I am not so old that I do not recall how the blood races when one is young. But you . . . I do not know . . . never have I seen one so careless for consequence. Your father wishes only the best for you. Why do you repay him with such foolishness, eh, Santiago? Think what an opportunity he presents you with! To be a doctor is a noble thing."

"I do not want to be a doctor. I want to be an artist."

"Oho!" He whistled. "No wonder your good papa loses patience with you. Artists are born to die in poverty."

I would have argued the point with him, for often I had stubbornly resisted my father's calm intellectualizing — such and such a man thought himself an artist but his paintings were ridiculed; writers persuaded themselves they were geniuses and wound up their humdrum existences scratching away at records in some county hall, etcetera, etcetera, etcetera — but we had now reached the jail. It was not until the rusty door screamed open and shut behind me, and the key was turned in the lock, that I at last believed this was in truth happening to me. I wrapped my fingers around the bars, staring stupidly after the constable's retreating figure. I could only think I am in prison, I, Santiago Ramón y Cajal, am actually in prison. And my father let them do this to me!

The sound of laughter shocked me from my trance. Peering in at me through a small grille were some of the smaller children of our village. "Hey, Santiago," a brave one called. "You choose a strange place from which to view the fiesta." The others giggled. Emboldened, he persisted, "Perhaps your father can arrange to exchange you for one of the infidel Moors, eh, Santiago? But what a punishment that would be for the enemy!"

Looking about me, I saw a stone lying near the window ledge. I grasped it tightly in my hand and said through my teeth, "I shall not be in this place forever, Carlos. When I am free, I shall seek you out and smash your brain from your tiny skull."

He wailed in sudden fright. He did not know that of course I would do no such thing; I would never willingly harm a living soul. His mother snatched him from the grille, first shouting down at me, "You are a devil, Santiago. You will rot in hell, regard my words." And she whisked him away, chasing the others before her as well. "Let him be, that he may contemplate what his evil ways have brought him to," her words floated back to me.

Now I took stock of my situation. Contemplation was indeed required, but not of my evil ways. The first thing I noted was my bed, which was a pallet of straw, moldy, alive with vermin, and emitting an unbelievable stench. I approached the pallet warily and kicked it. Several roaches ran from hiding and disappeared down a crack in the far wall. I went back to the window, trying to peer out, but night had already begun to fall. I could hear the sound of music. Mayor Pavía had arranged for a gypsy band to come and play for us. Gypsies often traveled through our area. Certainly no one in our village could play such an assortment of instruments, though my father was gifted in the strumming of the guitar and I myself have constructed flutes from cane, with all of the necessary stops and keys. I have made flutes with a range of two octaves whose quality even my father has commented upon favorably. Indeed, not often but at times my father has consented to our playing together. The flute and the guitar can create much beauty. It is too bad that we are not really musicians, my father and I. Perhaps there would have been some harmony in our lives.

There was dancing in the streets. I could hear the clicking of heels and the rhythm of snapping fingers. All would be gaily dressed — if not for a fiesta, then when? My mother, like the others, would be wearing a vivid skirt that would billow out as she danced. Her trim body would appear to advantage in a bright embroidered bodice. She would wear, also, no doubt, the beautiful flowered shawl my father had bought for her in Barcelona and her thick, black, long hair would be covered with the black lace mantilla he had purchased in Barcelona as well. How I longed to see her this way. She had so little occasion for dressing up.

I tired finally of straining to see through the small grille. With a last shaking of the door, to see if it had somehow come unlocked, I sought a clean area on the floor and stretched myself out despondently upon the tiles. I clasped my hands beneath my head and bleakly contemplated my future for the next few days. After a while, I dozed. Perhaps I slept more deeply than I thought, for a sound brought me to my feet, my heart thudding.

"Who is it? Who goes there?" I asked, confused. My cell was now in complete darkness.

"Pssst. Santiago. Shhhh. Do not raise your voice. It is I."

"Pedro! You should not be here. If father finds out, he will be very angry with you."

"Father has been called to Huesca. Listen, Santiago. I have brought you something to eat." Pedro stuck his hand through the bars of the window. "Here. Take it while it is still hot." It was a large, delicious chunk of fowl that had been baked over a huge bonfire in the square. "It is a fire of much magnificence," Pedro said, describing the scene to me. "Many sheep and fowl are being roasted. You can smell it everywhere." He lifted his head and breathed deeply. "And there is wine." I was familiar with how the wine is passed from one to the other in old leather bottles. Many a time I had been allowed to take a sip at the fiesta. There was much rough talk, all in good fellowship, and a happy boisterousness kindled on these occasions. And why not? The life of the Aragón peasant does not yield much gaiety. "Shall I bring you

33

more food?" Pedro asked. I could tell from his restlessness that he was anxious to get back to the fiesta. I understood. Would I not wish to do the same in his place?

"No more food. Only, Pedro, listen. I must occupy my time somehow. There is nothing in this accursed place! You cannot bring me a book; Father will not allow it. Bring me my paints."

"What will you paint on?"

"The walls. The floors," I replied brusquely. "I don't care. Just bring them, Pedro." Having promised, my brother slipped quietly away into the darkness and I once again settled myself upon the floor.

I could have real paints and real brushes, I thought bitterly, if my father did not despise me so. But such opposition only made me more stubborn. I improvised. My father smoked, making his cigarettes from little packets of cigarette paper. This paper came in bindings of bright red and dark blue. When he discarded the bindings, I retrieved them and soaked them, thus obtaining two primary colors for my paintings. Other times I simply scraped paint from the walls. Since I had no brushes, I was forced to improvise here as well. When I had extracted all the color from the bindings, I rolled them up and dampened them, and with these stumps I achieved some success. Most often, of course, I was obliged to draw only with my pencil.

I do not remember falling asleep. When I awoke sunlight was already streaming in through the grilled window, creating small blocks of light and shadow on the floor.

"So, lazy one. You are up at last? What it is to be young," the constable chuckled. "Once I, too, could have slept like a dead one on the hard floor. Now my old bones need the comfort of feathers and down. Are you hungry? Do not think of food. The time will pass somehow."

"Can you not bring me some breakfast?" I pleaded. Confinement to this squalid place had not affected my appetite, unfortunately. 2076938

"I? Go against the wishes of your father? The time will pass. Depend upon it." A shadow blocked the sun from the window. He glanced up casually and then away. "Well, I cannot stay and chat all day. I have my duties, you understand." With a last smiling glance at the window, he ambled away.

I went closer to the metal grating. A woman of ample proportions knelt at the window — small wonder she hid the sun! Her eyes were almost lost in the flushed, mounded flesh of her face, her nose was somewhat bulbous, and under it dark hair outlined her upper lip.

"Your mother has asked me to attend to you, Santiago," she wheezed. I must tell you that Doña Bernardina de Normante has been widowed twice, and has since remarried. If she were to be widowed a dozen times, there would be no lack of suitors for her stubby-fingered hand, for Doña Bernardina is a genius in the kitchen. It was almost worth being in jail to

35

sample her *sequillos* and *coscaranas*, those spice cakes that make my mouth water just to think of them.

I stuffed the food into my mouth greedily. "But Papa has forbidden that I be given food."

Doña Bernardina shrugged. "Don Justo has forbidden the jailer to feed you. Not one word did he utter to me." She laughed heartily. "I will go to confession on Sunday. Meanwhile, a growling stomach must be quieted."

"You are an angel of mercy, Doña Bernardina," I told her fervently.

"With such a one as me, the good Lord will have a problem in Heaven." She laughed again, rising with some difficulty from her knees. "This evening I will return with some chops and a pie. Be of good cheer, Santiago. Your good mother sends you her affection."

No sooner had she gone when Pedro arrived with my paints. He visited with me briefly. When he left, I regarded the rough walls of my cell. They were not too clean, nor were they of a texture suitable for painting, but they were bare and this was sufficient for my purpose.

For the next three days, I drew. One wall I devoted to scenes from the bullring — a *banderillero* driving a dart into a bull, a *matador* standing proud and alone, clasping his cape in one hand and readying his sword in the other, the bull pawing the ground. How good my painting was I could not judge. The constable studied the wall, moving from *banderillero* to *matador* to bull without comment. Later in the day he brought me a small paint brush and a can of paint, left over, he explained, from retouching his barn. When I thanked him, he said brusquely that the other walls could also stand some improvement.

Whatever turbulent scenes I recalled from books, from imagination, from the daily life about me, these I strove to put upon the walls. One I devoted to scenes of war, for, as I have mentioned, I was filled with the patriotic fervor of the times. Side by side with battles and falling soldiers, I drew people of the village going about their tasks — the farmer in the field, a woman making bread, a boy riding a mule.

Thus the days of my confinement passed slowly until at last the prison door swung open and I was free once again. Pedro was waiting for me when I emerged, his eyes anxious, his manner strained.

"Has something happened to Mama?" I asked in alarm.

"No, Santiago." His eyes filled with tears. "Something much worse." He swallowed. "Papa is home. And he is going to send you away."

FOUR

"Santiago," Pedro said urgently, "we must go home now. It is getting late. Papa will be very angry with us."

"I did not ask you to come to the woods with me," I replied shortly.

When Pedro had come to the jail with his news, I had refused to return home. Instead, I had fled to the woods, which were always to me a place of tranquillity, of gentle solitude, where my spirit could become whole again. I have a need often to be alone, to sort out my ideas, to *own* myself. This my friends and my parents do not comprehend. How shall I explain this to you? When someone speaks to you, then you must reply, is it not so? The words fly back and forth between you. Words provoke thoughts and emotions and perhaps even memories you may not wish to think or feel or remember. In conversation, your mind is engaged by someone else. Alone, your mind is free.

My mother, sweet, gentle woman that she is,

39

worries. "Santiago," she says, "it is not natural for one so young as you to be so much alone. What is it that you do by yourself all day long?"

"I explore the ravines, Mama, the springs, the rocks, the hills. I look upon sunlight touching the water. I listen to the river flowing by. I study the insects . . ."

"And if you have an accident," she interrupts. "If you fall and hurt yourself, eh, Santiago? What then?"

She does not understand. Nor does my father. He believes I hide in the woods to avoid what he calls my responsibilities. So I no longer try to explain. Not even to Pedro. Today was a perfect example. I truly did not wish my brother to come to the woods with me. After my four days in the *cárcel,* I needed more than ever to be here by myself, but Pedro would not leave my side. And he talked. I had flung myself down on the bank of our river, my hands clasped under my head; Pedro sat beside me and looked up at the foliage of the willow shading us from the heat of the sun.

"What bird is that?" he asked idly.

"A linnet."

"It is remarkable how you can identify the birds, Santiago."

"It is not so remarkable. One has only to look and listen. Be quiet, please, Pedro. I do not wish to talk now."

"As you say." Pedro lapsed into silence. But my brother is not one who is comfortable in such a situation, so presently he laughed. "Do you remember last year, when you were collecting birds' eggs, Santiago?"

40

I nodded. I remembered it very well. I have a great love for God's creatures. Last year I had offered the boys of the village a *cauderna* apiece for each nest they would find for me — not bad pay, a penny each, considering how rigid the economy is in our household. My father is, by village standards at least, a man of means. But he is a saving man. Perhaps it is because his own youth was so poor and the hardships he underwent to gain his schooling more severe than for most. My mother is a prudent housekeeper, and we are not spoiled by luxuries, either on the table or on our persons. So to obtain even a *cauderna* to pay for nests was for me most difficult.

"How many eggs did you collect?" Pedro asked.

"I think at least thirty different eggs." I had constructed a special pasteboard box that I had divided into small spaces. In each space, which I labeled most carefully, I placed the egg removed from the nest — the buff white egg of the lark, the blue white speckled egg of the thrush, the blue egg of the goldfinch . . . Would you believe that that summer cost me close to one hundred *cuudernas?* For naturally I had to pay even when the nest was a duplicate.

Pedro poked me. "Do you recall what happened to your collection? The stink! It was unbelievable!" I had to smile, remembering. Last summer was hot, as our summers are always hot. But in other summers I had not been a collector of eggs. How fiercely our Spanish sun burns! Inside the shells, the yolks wilted and decayed; the shells themselves cracked. Soon the stench from the eggs pervaded every corner of our

41

room. Days passed before the odor was finally gone. Until it passed, Pedro and I slept in the barn. My father was not pleased with this experiment, I can assure you.

But I was only thirteen then. It is much different now. This spring I favored trapping nestlings. Understand me, I was most careful in constructing my *lienas*, my traps. I made deep holes which I covered with small sticks loosely spread about which the bird, in nibbling at the bait I lured it with, could dislodge easily. When I brought a nestling home, I put it in a cage which I made myself. Sometimes I wove a cage from reeds. Other times I used twigs from the red osier, a willow whose branches and twigs are flexible but quite strong.

Do you know the joy of watching a bird grow? It is an enchantment, from the first show of the downy feathers to the first timorous testing of the wings. I do not keep my nestlings caged forever. I let them go always to seek the freedom of the skies.

I did not do this from a sense of cruelty — capturing the nestlings, that is. It was a matter of scientific observation, for I kept notes on all of my birds, and drew pictures of them in their various stages of growth. Suddenly I felt my eyes sting with tears. All this was now behind me. My life in Ayerbe was coming to a close. What plans did my father have for me?

I jumped up. "I suppose we must go home. I might as well find out what bright future Papa has in store for me."

"Maybe it will not be too bad," Pedro suggested,

running alongside of me. My brother lives with more hope than I. We arrived at our house, fortunately, just in time for the meal. My father frowned when we slipped into our chairs, but said nothing; merely bowed his head and began to say grace, something he does to please my mother, for my father is not a religious man. We ate in silence. Toward the end, when we put our knives and forks down finally, my father addressed himself to me.

"Attend me, Santiago. I have decided to send you away to school, to Jaca, to the order of the Esculapian fathers." I could feel myself growing pale. The reputation of this school had reached even our ears, here in Ayerbe. "Their ability to teach Latin is unequaled," my father continued. He did not need to add that their iron control over rebellious spirits was even better known. I looked around the table desperately. My mother avoided my glance, but I could see how her lips trembled.

"Papa," I pleaded. "I beg of you. Send me to Zaragoza instead. There is a fine school of art in Zaragoza. I promise you that if you let me go to Zaragoza, I will study hard. Besides," I added with some cunning, "would it not be a great waste of money and time when it is clear that I do not have a head for Latin and such studies?"

"Is this not possible, so long as Santiago faithfully promises to study hard, and change his ways?" my mother asked hopefully.

"Antonia, the arrangements have already been made."

43

"Please, Papa," I said frantically. "If I could but show you some of my drawings."

For a long moment my father remained silent; beneath the table, I clasped and unclasped my fingers in agonizing tension. Pedro looked down at his plate, afraid to move. Would my father grow even angrier because I had openly declared that I was still painting, even though he had forbidden it? My mother, too, waited, her eyes large and expectant.

"Very well," my father said finally. "Bring your drawings."

I flew up the steps, emptied the contents of the deep chest at the foot of my bed, and raced down again, my papers spilling from my arms. I could not judge if my art was good or bad, only that it came from deep within. Do you know what it is like, to wait at the seat of judgment? If I grow to be as old and folded in upon myself as Señor Paño, who sits in the public square in the shadow of the tower, staring blankly into space, spittle dribbling down his trembling lip into his sparse gray beard, this single moment with my father will never depart from my mind. One after the other he studied my drawings — my countrysides that might have been inspired by Dante's "Inferno" nestling side by side with the romantic valleys of my mind's eye; my feudal heroes with their shining armor and plumed helmets. Everything I had ever read was here on these papers — war scenes, sinking ships, drowning sailors, charging animals! When he came to the last of my drawings, I could stand it no longer.

"Papa?"

He shrugged. "I am no judge of such things." He spoke but the simple truth. He is a man who has perhaps worked harder and studied longer than most men. Yet there is in him no joy. Whatever is creative in life is to him either to be ignored or condemned. The flaming glory of a sunset to him is not beauty, merely the ending of the day. How then could my scratches on paper be meaningful to him? "To be fair," my father continued, "we must have someone who knows a little of art look at your work."

My mother glowed. "You will take them to Zaragoza, to the art school?"

My father shook his head. "There is not time to travel there and back before Santiago goes off to school in Jaca. But there is someone in the village who can help us."

"In our village?" I could not imagine who in our entire community this could be.

"Choose one of these drawings," my father replied with some impatience, "and we will hear what he says."

Which painting to take to this expert? Which painting to choose that would decide my fate? I was almost paralyzed with indecision. At last I seized upon a picture of Saint James, that patron of mother Spain and the despair of the Moors. Surely, he, who was also my own patron saint, would save me from Jaca and the Esculapian fathers. Leaving Pedro to collect and put away my drawings, I followed my father as he strode down the stepped streets toward the church.

"Father," I cried, leaping after him, "who in the village are we consulting?"

"You will see." And with that I had to be satisfied. When we arrived at the church, I expected to go inside, but my father halted, looked about, and then went around behind the building. There upon a ladder a short lean man was engaged in whitewashing the wall. He whistled as he applied the brush, a small hissing sound that escaped from his pursed lips like steam from a boiling kettle.

"Señor, *por favor*," my father called up to him. "We have a matter of some importance to discuss with you."

He descended the ladder with alacrity, whether it was because my father had put his request so urgently or that he welcomed a chance to stop working, I cannot say.

"I am at your service," he said, glancing curiously from my father to me and back again.

"Show him your picture," my father commanded me. I was hesitant. Was this the art expert, this man whom Mayor Pavía had hired to plaster and paint the walls of the church? "Well?" my father said.

I handed the paper to the painter, who now studied it as he had applied himself to the whitewashing, with pursed lips and a steady, monotonous whistle. He examined it, closed his eyes, opened his eyes, examined it again. My father regarded his antics with some disfavor, but he said nothing. At last, just as I was about to interrupt his posturing, he rubbed his nose solemnly and pronounced his verdict.

"This is your son? This young man aspires to be an

artist?" He called my father to his side, turning his back upon me. "Regard, Señor. These dabs of color." He shook his head. "And the draperies." He put his tongue behind his closed teeth and made a hissing sound. "This is an apostle? Observe the proportions. All wrong. Hopeless. Hopeless. Throw away his brushes, Señor, I beg of you. He will never be an artist."

I was stricken dumb.

"You are certain that he shows no talent for art?" my father inquired sternly.

"Throw away his brushes," the newly appointed art critic repeated. "That is my answer to you, Señor." He turned finally to me. "You, there, my poor, poor fellow. Have you no eyes in your head? Regard the hands you have inflicted upon this apostle! Such hands should be used for glove maker's samples! Regard his body. Why is it so short? And this horse. *Por favor, Señor*," he said, appealing to my father, "does such an animal exist? Only on a carousel, Señor, believe me."

Sick at heart, I seized my painting. "Who are you to judge, you . . . you dauber of walls!" I cried. Instantly my father slapped me across the side of my face for my insolence.

"You will apologize," he said coldly.

"Please, Señor," the painter said. "It is not necessary." But he did not know my father. I apologized but I did not forgive him, for with his words he had condemned me to the Esculapian fathers.

We returned to our home. My face obviously told

47

the story, for neither my mother nor Pedro questioned us. I started to go up to my room when my father called me back. "You will bring me your drawings," he said quietly. "All of them. You will likewise bring your pencils, your charcoals, your paints, and your papers. From this moment forward, you are to put behind you this foolishness and devote yourself to your studies. Is it understood?"

"It is understood," I replied, my voice leaden. While he methodically ripped my drawings and destroyed my paints, I stood stolidly by. My mother tried but once to interfere. "Please, Justo. Will you not reconsider?" She knew, even as she asked, that he would not.

"In two days time," he said, "we will depart for Jaca."

Thus was my fate decided.

FIVE

J<small>ACA</small>, which is to the north of Ayerbe, is
perhaps not so far from my village as it seemed the
morning my father and I left home. I had long since
bidden my friends farewell. José had pressed upon me
his precious goatskin sling; Lope gave me a fine sheet
of blank paper which he had rolled carefully so the
ends would not fray from handling. Claudio insisted
that I take a stubby pencil which had a deep, satisfying
blackness to the lead. Francisco and Juan had collected cigarette papers so that I would not lack for
colors. All these items I had hidden carefully among
my clothing.

Before I climbed into the carrier's cart, where my
father had already swung our baggage, my mother
came running out. She insisted that a mattress be
placed over the bags, for well she knew that to be
bumped endlessly over rough roads is to suffer much
nausea. I cannot honestly say that I was comfortable
on my perch at the very front end of the wagon, but I
was more occupied at first with my thoughts than with
the hardship of the journey. I wished that my mother

49

had not cried so hard; it had only made my father the more impatient.

"Antonia," he protested finally. "Santiago does not go to the end of the world. He goes no further than Jaca."

"You are right, Justo," she agreed miserably, pressing me to her. Wiping her tears, she attempted a small, wavering smile. "It is not so long a time until summer," she told me bravely. "Be of good cheer, Santiago."

"Not so long a time," I repeated. The month was now September, with the golden glow that September brings; I would not return to Ayerbe until the following summer. Not so long a time? It would be an eternity. From my place on the cart, I looked down upon her face. I could not even swallow. I did not dream that one can actually feel the weight of one's heart as a leaden mass in one's chest.

I did not see Pedro at all, at least not near the cart, but I knew he must be watching from the window of our room, so as the wagon creaked its way past our house, I turned and waved. I saw the curtain move slightly but there was no answering wave. Perhaps Pedro was crying; certainly his eyes had been red since they opened to this day of parting. I would have cried, too, but I would not shed tears in my father's presence.

The trip began in dead silence, save for the sound of the wagon wheels jolting along the rough surface and the rhythmic slapping of the horse's hooves against the road. From time to time, my father pulled his watch from his pocket, snapped open the lid, stared at the face of the timepiece as if it held some secret message engraved upon it, then closed the lid and replaced the watch.

The journey from Ayerbe to Murillo is of an unbelievable monotony; many times my eyes, growing weary of the aridity of the land, closed and my head nodded heavily. However, once past Murillo, the road follows the contours of the Gállego. It is a river of many moods, that Gállego, here placid and little more than a broad and shallow stream, there turbulent, hurling itself forcefully between huge boulders. Sometimes it stays in full view; other times it hides in narrow gorges. I do not know what it is within me that responds so to the sights and sounds of the river. Perhaps it is because man himself came from the sea in eons past.

I had resolved not to exchange a single word with my father, but now I could not help myself. When I gazed upon the mountain at Riglos, I exclaimed, "Papa! Those rock formations! They are like the columns of a palace of Titans!"

My father regarded the formations critically. "They appear more like mallets," he said. For my father, this was indeed exercising the imagination. "I know this area well," he continued, smiling. "I grew up in this region." While my eyes feasted on the scenery, he told me stories of the people hereabout, and things that had happened to him in his youth. Later he pointed out the great rock of Lapeña which looms over the village beneath it like a giant threat of disaster. Even the Gállego is subdued here, running quietly by

51

at the bottom of a deep ravine. When we reached Anzánigo, I could see to the west the gloomy peak of Mount Pano.

I was bone weary by this time, my body protesting each movement of the wagon. My father, I think, is a man of iron. Not by word or look did he show discomfort. When I sighed, he said drily, "Take courage, Santiago. Our journey is almost at an end. When you see the Uruel range, we will be approaching Jaca."

I do not know if you are acquainted with our Uruel Mountain. Its red peak rises over the valley of Jaca like the watchful Sphinx in the deserts of Egypt. When I did in fact see the mountain, I welcomed the sight as a Viking must have regarded Valhalla. It was not that I was anxious to be turned over to the Esculapian order; I wished only to leave the cart and walk upright again upon my own two feet.

"Is Uncle Juan expecting us?" I asked.

Uncle Juan is my mother's brother. He is, I suppose, a good man. Certainly he is hard-working, even though he is old. My mother tells me Uncle Juan is a skillful weaver, but fortune has not smiled upon him. He makes little money. He is a widower, his wife having died some years back. His children are gone from home, all but the youngest son, Timoteo, who refuses to help his father and has gone to work in a chocolate factory instead. An old, crotchety woman keeps house for him; she has no teeth and gums her food. In all the time I was to live with Uncle Juan her method of eating fascinated me. When she opened her mouth, it was like a black, gaping hole. To chew her food, she clamped her lips tight. They seemed to disappear into her mouth along with the food. Only her jaw worked in and out, back and forth.

When we arrived, however, Estrellita — how strange that this gnarled old woman should have a name so exquisite: Little Star — was not present, only my Uncle Juan, who left his loom with great reluctance.

My room was in the attic, a small, hot chamber with a bed, a shelf, and some hooks in the corner to serve as a closet for my clothing. From my window I could see the mountains and down across the valley. Since I suspected that housekeeping here would not be done in an overzealous manner, I felt safe in putting my baggage under the bed. Here, too, I would keep my drawings, for that I would continue to paint I did not doubt for a moment.

When I came down the stairs again, my father was eager to be off to the school so that he might meet the fathers and charge me to their care.

My first sight of the building did nothing to reassure me. It was like a fortress built not so much to withstand the shock of battle from without as to keep its inmates confined. When I saw it looming above me, I was chilled. I felt I was exchanging the discomfort of my cell in Ayerbe for a new, more confining, more punishing prison. My father was troubled by no such premonitions; he urged me forward. We were brought at once into the presence of the director of the school. The two men greeted each other with much respect. My father has great reverence for any man of learning; the abbot apparently had equal regard for a professional man.

"So this is Santiago." The abbot turned finally to me.

"He is in need of much discipline," my father told him. "I wish you to watch him carefully. And if he displeases you or his teachers, be assured that whatever punishment you give him, I will regard as coming from me."

"Ah," the abbot sighed. "If only our other parents had your understanding." He rang a small bell. Instantly the door opened, and a brother looked in inquiringly. "Send Father Jacinto to me," the abbot requested. The brother disappeared as silently as he had come. "Father Jacinto teaches elementary Latin," the abbot explained. "He is one of our finest teachers."

Father Miguel had taught me some Latin at home. He is small and dry and dusty, like the books from which he daily intoned our lessons. I think perhaps I expected to see another Father Miguel, so I was doubly unprepared for the friar who came striding into the room.

Father Jacinto is a giant of a man, as broad as he is tall, with a roaring voice that shakes the walls, and hands of an unbelievable size. After greeting my father, he turned his attention to me.

"So this is the young colt we have to break," he bellowed. "I know that look," he told my father, smiling. "Did you not see how he bridled at my

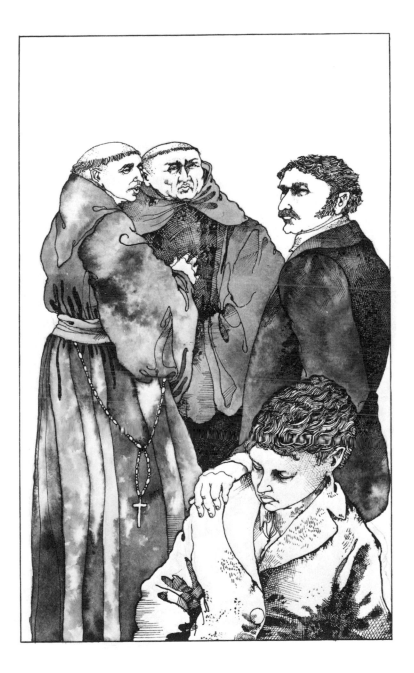

words? Have no fear, young master," he assured me. "I have broken the wildest horses to the saddle."

Far from being upset at these words, my father declared himself reassured. It was arranged that I would begin classes next day. Meanwhile we returned to the home of my uncle and to the evening meal.

"You are not to indulge him simply because he is your nephew," my father cautioned Uncle Juan. The old man regarded my father tiredly. Timoteo looked at me and winked. I did not understand why. How was I to know that our diet would consist of cabbages and turnips and potatoes with a piece of meat appearing only on feast days? Now Estrellita placed before me a dish of most unappetizing appearance. I pushed it about with my spoon.

Timoteo watched me a moment, then laughed. "What, cousin, you do not fancy *farinetas?*"

"It is cornmeal porridge," Uncle Juan advised me. "Eat it. It will stick to your ribs."

"You will come to like it in time," my father said, eating with appetite.

"That day will never come," I said under my breath. But I was wrong. Not too far in the future I would risk dire punishment at the school for a heaping bowl of this disgusting dish.

SIX

Do you know the story of Carthage, that city on the coast of North Africa that was established by the Phoenicians? It was like a bone in the throat of the Romans, who swore they would not rest until Carthage fell. One Roman senator, Cato by name, a man much given to speech-making, got into the habit of ending each oration with the words *delenda est Carthago* which, translated loosely, means Carthage must be destroyed.

To Father Jacinto, I was Carthage, and like Carthage I fell before his onslaught, save that for me it became a daily event. It began the next morning. I had risen early to bid good-by to my father who was anxious to return to Ayerbe.

"I will see you next summer," he told me hastily. I never believed that I would miss his presence so much! Alone, I made my way slowly to school. I entered the classroom as quietly as possible. Father Jacinto was seated on a bench placed upon a platform at the front end of the room, so that he towered like a colossus above the students. In his hands, he clutched a cat-o'-nine-tails. Immediately all eyes were upon me.

"I have the honor to present to you Santiago Ramón y Cajal," he said. The boys snickered. How we cowards love new victims! "Enter! Enter!" I could feel the door vibrating against my body from the force of his voice. "Sit there, beside Fernando." A small, slight boy with strangely light eyes beckoned to me. "You are now a Carthaginian," Father Jacinto announced.

I stared at him blankly.

"The room is divided into Carthaginians and Romans," Fernando whispered. In other words, the losers pitted against the winners. It was a notion to please the giant who held us in his huge hands. The cat-o'-nine-tails snaked out. Aiming for Fernando, it hit me instead. Father Jacinto smiled. "No matter, Santiago," he purred. "You will be deserving it soon enough."

Thus the war began. Each day my body dutifully took its place beside Fernando; my mind, however, fled from the classroom. Father Jacinto raged and whipped and raged again.

"*Estúpido! Estúpido! Estúpido!*" he gritted at me through his teeth.

Perhaps he was right. I am not one who has quickness in the use of words; I cannot spill back instantly what I have learned. My father, however strict a teacher he was for me, understood this. He did not expect me to repeat word for word my lessons, only that I absorb and then explain what I absorbed. So I began to reason, if I am indeed stupid, why should I even try? Therefore, I once more began, as I had done with Father Miguel, to draw in the margins of my books. True, these margins were not so wide or satisfactory as those in the catechism, but the space was white and clear.

One morning I looked up from my drawing to find Father Jacinto bending over me. It was so rare for him to move from his throne up forward (I was well seated in the back of the room) that I was startled.

"So," he said, "it would appear that you have given up the study of Latin to devote yourself to scribbling." He took the book from my nerveless hand and held it aloft. "Is it any wonder Carthage fell?" he asked the students. Obediently they giggled. "While the Romans progress, this Carthaginian sits and idles. I think perhaps he enjoys the feel of the whip." The students waited; better me than they. And why not? It is possible to be very brave in the face of another's pain. Only my little friend Fernando, who lived in mortal terror of Father Jacinto, showed the heart of a lion.

"Please, Father," he begged in a low voice, his light eyes at once both terrified and determined. "See how his wrists swell . . ."

Father Jacinto lifted Fernando, plucking him from his seat effortlessly, and held him in the air. "A lesson you must learn, Carthaginian," he said, and the calmness of his face was more threatening than if it had been contorted with his usual anger, "is the value of minding your own business." With that, he flung Fernando against the blackboard some seven feet across the room. The blackboard shattered and fell; Fernando lay crumpled and silent on the floor. I ran

59

to his side, examining him as I had seen my father's hands move gently over a patient.

I had never before realized that hate can be a living, physical thing; I could feel it exploding within me like a volcanic eruption. It raced along my veins and boiled into my brain. Purple and red spots danced before my eyes; my head felt as if it were about to burst. I seized the cat-o'-nine-tails and lashed out at Father Jacinto, catching him across the arms and chest. And into this scene walked the abbot. He stood, shocked, in the doorway. I had raised the whip to strike again, but I was no Father Jacinto; I had no taste for the whip. I let my hand fall. The abbot spoke. "Pray, Santiago," he whispered. "Pray for your immortal soul."

"It is not my soul that concerns me," I replied in white heat. "It is my body. I will not be whipped again. If Father Jacinto beats me one more time, I will run away and stay away."

"Have no fear. He will not touch you again," the abbot said coldly. "I think there are better ways to teach a boy discipline."

Fernando moaned and sat up. I helped him to his feet and walked with him to the door, determined to bring him to his room that he might rest. Not one word was spoken. Father Jacinto stood where he was at my desk; the abbot remained in the open doorway. I thought at first that he meant to block our passage, for he did not move to let us by. I looked at him. Perhaps there was about me the coldness of my father, for after a moment he stepped aside and Fernando and I walked through.

"This is a colt that will take much breaking," I heard Father Jacinto say as Fernando and I left.

"He will be broken, Father," the abbot replied. "You have my word. He will be broken."

SEVEN

IF IT WERE NOT for life at school, I could have been most happy in Jaca. Do you know the beauty of this place? I think in all the Pyrenees there is no valley to equal it, surrounded as it is on all sides by the majesty of our mountains. I had but to look to the north to see el Pirineo towering to the sky, its peak covered always with snow, or to the south where the cruel Uruel, red and menacing, held back the breezes from the valley. From my attic window, glancing west across Jaca and the fertile fields which lay beyond it, I could see Mount Pano. To the east there were the mountains of Biescas; here, too, snow kept the peaks of Panticosa and Sallent perpetually white.

Rivers and mountains I tried again and again to capture in my drawing book, but I was never satisfied. At times I would throw my pencil away and swear I was finished but then a scene of beauty would pierce my heart and I would try again.

Timoteo came to my room once and caught me at

my work. He looked at my drawing, then out the window.

"That is supposed to be Mount Pano?" he asked, jerking his thumb toward my paper.

"I am trying."

"It is not bad. Tell me something, Santiago. Why do you wish to draw the mountain?"

"It is so beautiful, Timoteo. Look how it stands against the evening sun."

Timoteo shrugged. "It is no different now from what it is any other time the sun sets," he replied, puzzled. Then he laughed. "If you would work so hard at your studies as you do at this foolery, you would be something of a scholar."

"I am not a scholar, Timoteo. I am too stupid."

"How do you know this?" he asked.

"I cannot remember anything I study," I confessed. "Father Jacinto is right in this. I am stupid."

"Then why do you not leave school and come and work in the chocolate factory with me?" he urged kindly. "It is a good place and the work is not too difficult. Maybe at first it would be hard for you, for you are not so strong as I, but I would help you."

"You are good to me and I thank you . . ."

"*De nada,*" Timoteo interrupted.

". . . but I do not think I wish to work in the chocolate factory, if you do not mind."

Once again Timoteo shrugged. "I suppose a man must go his own way." He glanced out the window a last time. "He draws Mount Pano," he said to no one in particular, left the room, poked his head in the door and grinned, saying, "At least you will not run out of mountains while you are here in Jaca," then disappeared down the steps.

Next morning I discovered what Father Jacinto and the abbot had devised for "breaking the colt." My new punishment was hunger. A record of my misdeeds was kept in a special book. This record was joyfully inscribed by Victoriano, leader of the Carthaginians and second only to Father Jacinto in command of our miserable troupe. I will tell you the truth. Perhaps Victoriano had some reason to dislike me, for he and I had battled often enough on the school grounds. Victoriano was not one to fight honestly with his fists. Instead he noted each infraction of the rules of his fellow students and wrote them in the book which he showed to Father Jacinto at the end of the day. What extra beatings we received, thanks to Victoriano! Such a list was mine that Victoriano needed a book for me alone.

As I say, my new punishment was to be starvation. Each day, as soon as lessons were finished, Father Jacinto, or sometimes Victoriano, locked me in the classroom. Here I was bidden to stay, without food or drink, until the evening hour when it was time to return to my uncle's house. How I dreamed about the fruit José and Lope and Francisco and the rest of us in Ayerbe had stolen from the orchards! I even longed for Estrellita's lumpy, coarse dish of *farinetas*; in my longing, it became ambrosia, food fit for the gods!

Weeks passed; winter came and, with it, icy winds

from the north and the thick layering of snow. Now I wished even more desperately to escape from this new prison, to eat, and to join the others in the winter games. One day, after the key had made its familiar click in the lock, I decided I must break loose from this room. After examining the lock, I cast about me for some contrivance to force it. I searched Father Jacinto's bench — it had a small drawer — but found nothing but chalk. The other desks likewise yielded no tool. I paced the room, hitting the walls, went to the window and stared out, then returned to my own seat. From habit, I picked up my pencil and began to scribble. Suddenly I found myself staring at the pencil.

"Santiago," I addressed myself. "Can a pencil not be a lever?"

I ran to the door. I had no fear of making noise; the friars were attending some banquet or other, this being a feast day. I worried at the lock like an animal at a bone. When my pencil broke, I seized another. If I were so persistent in my studies, I would truly be a scholar! At last the spring in the lock yielded; the bolt slid open. Cautiously I opened the door, peering up and down the corridor. No one was in sight. I fled joyously from the building and to my uncle's house like a bird to its nesting place.

"Estrellita! Estrellita!" I burst in upon her. *"Por Dios!* Some food!"

She stared at me with some suspicion. "What? Are you home for lunch again after all this time?"

"You will see me here every day," I vowed.

"Quickly, Estrellita. I am starved." She did not know that I spoke but the simple truth.

"There is only some cabbage . . ." she began. I did not let her finish.

"Cabbage! Estrellita, I would give my soul for some cabbage."

She went out of the room, muttering, and when she came back, she thrust the dish before me ungraciously, but it was hot and filling. Seeing me scoop the food ravenously to my mouth, she went out again and returned with a generous portion of *farinetas*. I seized her hand and kissed it. She yanked it from me, saying, "You are as one possessed," crossed herself and left the room, but that evening I found a small cake by my bed.

Thus began my daily escape from the locked classroom. Uncle Juan accepted my presence at the table as indifferently as he accepted my absences. If he noticed that now and then Estrellita gave me an extra portion or fed me a piece of pastry, he said nothing.

One day as I shot the bolt of the classroom door and peered out, I stared straight into Father Jacinto's bull-like chest. He placed his huge hand on my head and spun me around like a top.

"So!" he said. "Our Santiago plays games. Let us see who is better at game playing." He forced me back into the classroom. As soon as the other students returned, he summoned Victoriano to his side. "Our Santiago," he announced to the class, "will now be our *rey de gallos*." King of the roosters! Can you understand the humiliation of this punishment? Victoriano ran to the closet and withdrew a ludicrous robe which Father Jacinto forced me to put on. In addition, Victoriano placed upon my head an enormous, tall, pointed hat covered with multicolored feathers. No Indian of the far-off Americas looked so wild as I.

"Now then, Victoriano," Father Jacinto said. "Be so good as to parade Santiago throughout the school. Let everyone hail our *rey de gallos.*"

Inside, my heart cried out against this attack upon my pride, but I would not let Father Jacinto and the others know my true feelings. He made of me a *bufón,* a clown? *Bueno!* I would be one truly. I crowed and made other rude noises, so that Father Jacinto, despite his promise never to touch me again, reached out in rage and slapped me across the neck. Thus I went off to allow everyone in the school to stare and mock, and so I spent the remainder of the day, king of the roosters.

Naturally the lock on the door was changed; I expected this, as I expected that I would be watched from that moment on. Once again I disappeared from my uncle's table at the noon hour. I did not try to spring the lock again. To begin with, Victoriano was ever on guard on the other side of the door, and I knew, from examining the lock, that it was no simple mechanism I could attack with a pencil.

One evening no one came to unlock the door. I saw the sun hurry to the western horizon, cast its dying radiance across the sky, and sink from sight. Night came quickly; the room grew dark and cold. I banged on the door. "Some one there! Anyone!" I shouted.

"Let me out." I put my head against the door and listened intently. "Victoriano," I cried desperately, "*por favor,* open the door or I will open your head for you!" Silence. I ran to the window and attempted to peer out. Nothing. No movement. No sound. Only the cold and the darkness. I had been forgotten. I wandered about the classroom until I grew weary, then stretched out upon a bench, huddled my knees to my chest for some warmth, and at last fell into fitful sleep. Every now and then I woke to the sounds of my stomach rumbling. When I opened my eyes again, sunlight was filtering through the window. Soon the door opened and Father Jacinto entered.

"What?" he said, staring. "Have you been here all night?"

"Please, Father, may I go home?" I asked. "I have had no food since yesterday morning's breakfast."

"To the benefit of your immortal soul," he replied sternly. "You may leave, as usual, at the dinner hour." That day I was more stupid than ever during class. When Father Jacinto asked me to decline *quisnam, quaenam, quodnam,* I could only look at him blankly. As soon as class was over and the door locked, I ran to the window.

Have I mentioned to you that the classroom was on the second floor? The window, which was tall and narrow, looked out upon the garden. I stuck my head out the window and studied the wall. It presented a smooth surface. To leave by the window, I would have to jump. If I jumped, I would most certainly break a few bones and, possibly, my neck. But how else was I to escape from this room, which daily became more hateful to me? I puzzled over the wall. There must be a way to scale it! There must!

You will not believe the simplicity of the plan that occurred to me at last! That night, after Uncle Juan and the others had gone to bed, I sneaked from the house, taking with me a number of spikes and a knife.

EIGHT

I DID NOT THINK Uncle Juan would notice that the spikes were gone from the barn, or that Estrellita would miss one small knife. Fortunately for my plan, the moon rode full and high in the sky.

I walked quickly back to the school, coming in through the garden behind the institution. I climbed the garden wall with the help of the sturdy vines that clung to it, jumped down on the other side, and crept along the tree-lined paths until I came directly under the window of my classroom, where an arbor rose gracefully near the wall of the school. With a quick glance about me, I took my knife from my pocket and began slowly and carefully to scrape away at the mortar between two bricks. When there was sufficient space, I drove in one of the spikes, using my shoe as a hammer, the tap-tap-tap of my shoe echoing in the still night. I stopped often to look all around, but no shout of discovery rent the quiet hour of the night; I was truly alone.

I climbed the arbor a little higher and repeated the

process, scraping mortar, digging a hole, driving in a spike. Here and there on the wall, I scraped and left the places bare. These crevices I expected to use as footholds. At last I was finished. I dropped to the ground and stared upward. The spikes were barely noticeable. I stood there smiling to myself, proud of my improvised ladder. In a moment, however, I heard some small sound. Prudently I raced for the shadow of the trees, back along the paths to the garden wall, over and down, and triumphantly back to my room.

Next day I did not look enviously at the retreating backs of my fellow students as they marched from the room to go to lunch. Anyone can walk through a door, I told myself gleefully. I could hardly wait to hear the bolt slip into place. I ran to the window and studied the grounds with a searching eye. No one was about; indeed, who would wish to stand watch over a garden, particularly at the hour of eating?

I opened the window slowly, fearful lest it make some betraying sound, but it moved up smoothly. I climbed out the window, my foot fumbling for the first spike. As I held firmly to the window ledge, my other foot reached for one of the crevices. My homemade ladder worked. Using the crevices and the spikes, I dropped at last to the ground, ran along the paths in the shadow of the trees, swung up and over the garden wall, and burst in upon my uncle and Estrellita just as they were sitting down at the table.

"What?" Uncle Juan asked in surprise. "Cannot those friars make up their minds? First you are here; then you are not. Now you are here again."

"You do not think they really wish me to starve?" I asked, reaching across the table — do you know how beautiful a dish of potatoes, steaming, with melted butter golden upon them, can be? — heaping a large portion upon my plate. I ate until I felt I would burst, taking no time to chat. But it did not matter. My uncle Juan is a man of few words; he does not regard conversation during mealtime as necessary or even of much interest. He works hard, that one. A moment away from his loom is a moment wasted. Eating does not bring in income.

As soon as I finished, I jumped to my feet.

"*Con su permiso, Tío,* I must return at once to school."

Uncle Juan raised his eyebrows in astonishment.

"With my permission?" he asked. "You wish to return at once to school? At once?" He rose from the table, muttering to himself. "What is one to believe? They tell me he is wild, that he behaves himself badly in school, and here he is, barely able to contain his eagerness to return to school."

I did not answer; I had learned that no one answers my uncle, nor does he expect it. Timoteo never listens, and Estrellita concerns herself only with preparing meals of the most reasonable nature.

Racing back to school, I had more than enough time to make my way back to my classroom and my seat, even to appear to be studying my book when the door opened and I glanced up innocently to see who would be first to enter. Thus a matter of days passed. Father Jacinto was troubled. I seemed to him to be too serene of mind. Surely a boy suffering from hunger should be

72

broken by this time. But I continued my stubborn way; indeed, perhaps I grew worse, for now I did not care whether I learned or not.

It was poor little Fernando who brought matters to a head for me. One day he was imprisoned with me for some little infraction of a rule. When the door closed behind our classmates, Fernando began to cry.

"I hate this place," he sobbed. "I have written to my father to come and take me away."

"It is not too bad, Fernando," I tried to console him. "Just think. Next year when you return, you will no longer have Father Jacinto for a teacher. Father Alfonso has a kind and generous nature. So also does Father Joaquín . . ."

"Will you come back, Santiago?" he interrupted.

"It is different with me," I replied slowly. "You they do not treat badly, Fernando, only as they do the others. But the abbot and Father Jacinto have sworn they must break me as a wild colt, and they will not rest until they do it. I cannot let them do this to me, Fernando. I do not know why this is so important to me, but I cannot let them do this."

"You are not like the others, Santiago. I knew that from the first."

"No," I said shortly. "Would that I were." I paced the room restlessly. With Fernando in the room, I could not go out the window. My stomach was rumbling. "Listen, Fernando," I said, turning away from the window, "how long will you have to go without lunch?"

"Two weeks. I punched Victoriano in the stomach,

but it was well worth it," he confessed, pleased with himself.

Two weeks! Two weeks without food again! "Fernando, if I tell you a way we can get our lunch and not be found out, do you swear never to tell a living soul?"

"I swear it!"

I took him to the window. "I will go first, to show you the way. Then you come after. I will wait at the foot of the wall until you are safely down. Then we will go to my uncle's house. I am sure he will not mind if I share my food with you."

Fernando looked down doubtfully. Of course he is much smaller than I; perhaps the distance appeared much greater to him. He drew back. "I'm afraid."

"Look, Fernando. I will show you how easy it is." I swung my feet out the window, went down my makeshift ladder quickly, and climbed up again. "See?"

"I'm sorry, Santiago. I am afraid."

I came back into the room. "Very well. Let us sit and talk. I know. I will draw a picture of you."

"You are disappointed in me," he said sadly. "You are ashamed to have such a coward hold you back."

"I would be ashamed," I replied with some anger, "if you think that I measure friendship by such small things as this."

We said nothing more. I made him sit by the window so that I could sketch him with the sun upon him, his face half-lit, half in shadow. To capture the strange shading of his eyes was particularly difficult. Thus, completely absorbed in what I was doing, it was not until I felt Father Jacinto's hand heavy upon me that I realized we were no longer alone.

Next day, when Fernando and I were locked in, he said at once, "It is my fault you were punished yesterday. If I had gone down the wall with you, you would not have drawn the picture and Father Jacinto would not have made you *rey de gallos* again." I shrugged my shoulders, but Fernando would not accept my indifference. "Today is not yesterday, Santiago. Today I will go down."

I tried to persuade Fernando that he owed me nothing, but he would not listen, only insisting that we go out the window as quickly as possible. At last I went to the window, swung out, and made my way quickly to the garden below. I waited. Fernando stuck his head out. As if his heart beat in my body, I could almost feel how it raced. First his legs emerged. Then, as I had done, he felt for the spikes with his feet, holding on to the window ledge.

"*Espléndido!*" I called, encouraging him. Slowly, slowly, he descended, till at last he stood beside me. Now indeed we moved swiftly, for there was not too much time to run to the house of my uncle, eat, and return. My uncle grumbled, as I suspected he would, but since I shared my food, he did not make too much of it. We ran all the way back to school.

"You go up first, Santiago," Fernando said. "I must wait a moment to catch my breath."

Giving the matter little thought, and being anxious to return to the classroom before the others, I scrambled up the wall. "Quickly. Quickly," I shouted down as soon as I was safely through the window. Fernando stood as if his feet had taken root, staring up at me. "I cannot come up, Santiago. The window is so far from the ground."

"Climb, I beg you, Fernando. Regard. You have only to look up at me, and not down at the ground. I will hold my hands out so you can grasp them . . ."

It was no use, for he would not move even when I offered to come down and push him up from behind. You can well imagine the scene when Father Jacinto returned to the classroom. His rage was such as threatened to explode in his head; this I could see from the purple red flush that started near his throat and spread over his face. Even his eyes grew red. So must a bull in the ring appear to the *toreador*, the mean, angered eyes in the lowered head, the hoof pawing the ground.

Instructing Victoriano to take charge of the class, Father Jacinto marched me to hurl me bodily before the abbot.

"He is not a boy," he shouted, "but an animal, a stubborn mule. Such a one I would put in a cage on bread and water . . ."

"Slowly, slowly," the abbot advised, sighing. "What new mischief has Santiago presented us with now?" He sat in silence while Father Jacinto related my newest outrage against discipline.

"You may return to your class," the abbot told Father Jacinto when he was finished speaking. "Santiago will remain here." When Father Jacinto began to protest, the abbot regarded him steadily until at last

Father Jacinto turned and left the room. For a long moment, the abbot said nothing. Then he spoke so softly, I had to strain to hear him. "Santiago, can you not try to understand what your father wishes for you? To study medicine, you must acquire an education. You are not altogether stupid. Why can you not be like the other boys at the school? Apply yourself to your lessons. Study hard. Many of our students become professional men when they leave our school. It is true that the first year in our school is hard. But life is hard, Santiago. We prepare our students for life."

"By beating them?" I asked sullenly.

"Boys need to be beaten," he replied with some surprise. "Does not your father whip you when you need it? Do not the fathers of your friends beat their sons when it is necessary?" He did not wait for my confirming nod. "My father whipped me often enough. Oh, yes, Santiago. I, too, know the taste of the cat-o'-nine-tails. To be chastised and scourged is important, for the thoughts of growing boys are often evil. Boys are like wild animals; for the good of their souls, Santiago, they need to be tamed."

The abbot rose from his seat and went to the window. I waited anxiously, not knowing what new torment would now be devised. Finally, he turned back to me.

"I have decided. A disciplinary court will be formed. The court will decide what will be done with you. You may go home to your uncle's house now, Santiago. You will be summoned."

77

NINE

My MOTHER HAD WEPT when I left home to go to school in Jaca. She wept even harder when I returned to Ayerbe.

"What have they done to you?" she asked, her throat constricted with tears.

"Mama, do not concern yourself," I said, smiling. "It is only a matter of a few pounds lost."

My father had said nothing when he saw me, the day he came to Jaca to take me away finally from the Esculapian fathers. What words he had with the abbot, he did not tell me and I did not ask. The day the abbot had threatened me with the disciplinary court I had gone to the house of my uncle and had thereafter steadfastly refused to return to the school. I had written my father a passionate letter, saying that if he forced me to remain a moment longer at the school in Jaca I would run away or kill myself. Perhaps the words looked stronger on the page than I realized, for my letter brought my father to Jaca, and me home again to Ayerbe. Now I reassured my mother. I admit that I appeared painfully thin: the bones on my face had become angular, my eyes had begun to sink in my head. I had been growing all this while, and the growing without sufficient food gave me the look, my mother said to my father (and for the first time I heard sharpness in her voice when she spoke to him), of one dying of consumption.

"We shall fatten you, Santiago." She hugged me to her. "Have no fear."

Spring and Ayerbe! It was a beautiful time for me, reunited as I was with my brother and my friends. I ran wilder than ever, for I could not seem to fill my heart enough with the sights and sound of freedom. I was as one drunk with the joy of it. But the school at Jaca had affected me more than I knew, for I found that even more often than before I wished for solitude and would sneak away from José and Lope and the others, even from Pedro, though I knew that this hurt him.

"Where do you go and what do you do?" Pedro asked me at last, after I had once again slipped away. "How is it that you go off to some lonely place, always by yourself? Are we not friends anymore?"

How to explain to my brother the difference between lonely and alone? Pedro is like my mother — have I not said this before? Like her, he must have people near, the sound of humanity at work and at play. To Pedro, to be by oneself is to be lonely. To be lonely is a great unhappiness. I have also been lonely and I know this well. But to be alone — ah, that is another matter, for then one can renew acquaintance with one's soul, come in harmony with one's spirit.

"You may come with me if you wish," I said in answer to Pedro's question. "But I do not think you will find what I am doing now of much interest to you, Pedro."

"Why not? Perhaps I can even help you."

"But I am only drawing. How can you help me with this? Look here, Pedro." I showed him a large sketchbook. "I am making a study of colors in nature."

Pedro looked at the sketchbook doubtfully.

"I do not understand what it is you are doing," he said at last, handing the book back to me.

"It is simple. Tell me, how do you describe the color green?"

"Green?" he repeated with surprise. "Green is . . . green. I suppose you mean light green, or dark green?"

"The leaves of the olive tree are a delicate silver green," I began, sounding, I suppose, much like my father when he informs us concerning one subject or another, "but the leaves of the weeping willow are a dark green with whitish coloring on the underside. The pine has a gray green cast; the boxwood is yellow green."

"And this is what you put in your book? The colors of green?"

"Not only green, Pedro. I am making for myself a picture dictionary of colors. See how I have arranged this? I am making a scale of colors. And next to each color, in all its different shadings, I am going to put a picture, a rock, or an insect, or a flower, or leaf."

"That is very interesting, Santiago," Pedro said, but I could see that he did not truly find it so, for he did not ask to accompany me again when he saw me leave the house with the sketchbook in my hands. Francisco, Juan, and the others also learned that the sketchbook was a signal that I desired to be alone. They were good friends and soon came to respect my wish, although they could not really understand this preference for solitude.

As it happened, however, they were caught up in an adventure which afterward we called the affair of the rose. And it began in this manner. I had drawn a sufficiency of wild flowers; now I turned my attention to the cultivated blossoms in the gardens, painting hyacinths, and pansies, and other such blooms. Unfortunately, most of the flowers I wished to paint were not those I could simply pluck from fields or the gardens of friends. The most beautiful of all, of course, were cultivated in the grounds of the palace of the marquis in the square. How to obtain samples? Did one knock on the door and ask to pick flowers? Do you see my dilemma?

I discussed this with Pedro and my friends, and instantly the matter was resolved.

"The flowers you need are at the palace?" Juan asked. "Then we must go to the palace and get them."

"Agreed," said Lope. "But I think we must not go during the daylight hours but rather when night has fallen."

"The gardeners at the palace are not gracious," Francisco said, smiling. "However, they retire early. I think if we go at ten o'clock, we will not need to disturb them."

It was like old times when we plotted our raids to the orchards. The solitariness of my painting they could not understand, but the promise of such an adventure appealed to all of us, to myself no less than to them.

The next night Pedro and I waited until all was still in the house; I was for climbing out the window, since I now considered myself somewhat experienced, but Pedro elected for the steps. We thought at first that we would be caught out even before we had started, for suddenly the door to my parents' room swung open and we could see our father silhouetted there. However, after listening intently a moment, he closed the door. Pedro and I moved like phantoms down the rest of the steps, and took care to melt in the shadows as best we could once we were outside.

As agreed, José, Francisco, Juan, Lope, and Claudio were already gathered in the square. How much larger it seemed in the darkness! We held a whispered conference; then, having decided our plan of action, we stole around the palace to the gardens in back which were protected by a high wall. A high grape trellis rose above the wall, with here and there vines of climbing roses, the flowers, clustered together, sweetly scenting the night air, but the thorns sharp and difficult to dislodge if they broke off in one's fingers. When we scaled the wall, I heard Claudio mutter.

"Be careful of the thorns," I whispered.

"I wonder if the *guardias* are asleep," Pedro said

uneasily. He is never too comfortable on these raids.

"One way to find out," Lope said, and before we knew what he was doing, he was tossing small pebbles on the roof of the gardeners' cottage.

"*Estúpido!*" Francisco cursed. "Do you wish to invite trouble?"

"If they are awake, they will come to the door. If they do, then we will wait until they go back to bed again. But if they do not come, then we will know they are snoring their heads off, and we can help Santiago choose the flowers he must have for his great project."

"It is not a great project, Lope . . ."

"Sh-h-h! *Silencio!*" Claudio said. "I hear something."

We strained to hear, but the night gave back to us only the thumping of our own hearts and the sound of Claudio swallowing. When Claudio is under stress, he has this habit of making great swallowing noises, but we are so used to this that we do not notice it any more.

"It is safe," Lope announced. "Let us now continue with our mission."

"The flowers are so beautiful, it is hard to decide which ones to take," I confessed.

"*Por amor de Dios,*" Pedro pleaded with me, "choose and let us leave this place."

"I will have such a home one day," Francisco said dreamily, as he watched me choose a blossom with care. "Perhaps I shall even buy this palace from the marquis. Then you will come through the front door, Santiago . . ."

"And who will be your servant, eh, Francisco?" Lope, overhearing, demanded. "María Ruíz? Or perhaps her donkey?"

"Why not?" Francisco replied airily. He bent over and hobbled as María Ruíz did when she walked among the villagers in the square. "Enter," he imitated her high, shrill voice. "Enter, Santiago, the señor awaits you in his private gardens. Tell me, Santiago, is it true that you are world-famous as an artist?" Francisco cackled. "Hee-hee-hee! And to think I knew you when you wiped your nose with the back of your hand. Hee-hee-hee!"

Watching Francisco, we forgot for the moment where we were and the need for silence. We burst into laughter, all except Pedro, who cried out, "The *guardias!* I hear them coming!"

The two guards were indeed racing toward us, brandishing sturdy sticks in the air, strong, sturdy men, both of them, made even stronger by outrage at our having invaded their property. We had wandered too far from the spot where we had scaled the wall to enter the garden; the formidable iron gates were closed tight. How were we to escape our pursuers?

"We must race around and around the garden walks till we tire them." I suggested this quick strategy, and, so saying, I started off. The others came pelting behind me. Around and around we went in the maze of garden paths, running at full speed. But the *guardias* were tireless. Who would believe that men of such ageD Tomás, the older of the two, was at leastforty years — could have such endurance?

I ask you to picture how we must have appeared — seven boys and two men dashing madly about in a garden, the moon above shining serenely down upon us, and all about us the world asleep. I could not help myself; the situation was so ludicrous that I began to laugh. Lope, hearing me and understanding some little of what was passing through my mind, also began to choke with laughter. Have you ever tried to run and laugh at the same time? One can do one or the other but not both, for there is not enough breath in the body. Soon Lope and I were lagging behind the others; the *guardias* were gaining on us.

I looked up hopelessly at the high walls surrounding us. Time and again we passed the spot where we had entered. Unfortunately we needed time to climb, and this we did not have. At last, when it seemed that we could no longer keep up this insane milling about, an idea burst upon me. As we turned the corners of the paths, we were momentarily lost to the view of our pursuers. I had noticed that the branches of an apple tree swooped down at one point over the wall.

"Lope," I said urgently, "attend me. When next we pass this tree" — Lope looked up and nodded — "leap for the branch. Do you understand?" He nodded again. "I will tell the others. You go first."

Again we moved swiftly along the paths. This time, however, I ran side by side with each of my friends, one after the other, to tell them of my plan. "I am too short," Pedro objected. "I will not be able to reach the branch."

"You will reach it," I promised.

So we carried out my scheme. When we once again passed from view, Lope made a tremendous leap in the air. Catching the branch, he swung up and crawled along the branch like a cat. I could not hear him drop to the other side, for I kept on running. But a huge grin covered my face. Where there had been seven, there were now only six. Soon Francisco, Juan, then José and Claudio followed Lope. All disappeared over the wall as if the night had swallowed them.

Momentarily the *guardias* stopped in their tracks.

"The devil take them," Tomás swore. "Are they hiding?"

"If so, we will soon roust them out," the younger man said positively. "There are not so many hiding places that I cannot find them."

"Now!" I said to Pedro.

"It is too high," he panted.

"Jump. I will push."

Pedro sprang upward. His hand brushed the branch but his fingers closed about air. He fell back.

"You go, Santiago. I told you I couldn't reach it."

I glanced behind me apprehensively. "Run, Pedro. They are coming."

"I cannot move," he sighed. "How can such old men still run when I am already exhausted?" he added plaintively. I thought perhaps he would remain where he had fallen, but fear gave him new energy. Once again we sped around the garden. This time when we neared the apple tree, I was able to boost Pedro to the branch. I heard Claudio whisper, "I have him, Santiago. Save yourself."

"Aha, you miserable *ladrón*," a voice said almost in my ear. "I do not know where the others have got to, but here is one!"

I squirmed in Tomás's grasp. "I am not a thief," I protested. To call me a *ladrón* for a few flowers seemed very harsh.

"Who is it?" the other *guardia* asked, peering into my face.

"Who else but the son of our good doctor, Santiago Ramón y Cajal?" Tomás replied grimly. "No, idiot!" he exploded as his companion lifted his stick to beat me. "Do not thrash him. Let us give his father that pleasure."

So once again I was returned to my father in disgrace.

TEN

"WHEN THE NEW SCHOOL TERM begins," my father announced at the table next morning, "Santiago and Pedro will attend the Institute at Huesca."

Pedro and I exchanged glances. "You mean I am to go to school with Santiago?" Pedro's expression was joyous. My mother, too, was pleased. But my father soon laid our pleasure to rest.

"You will not be in the same classes, naturally," my father continued. "Nor will I permit you to stay at the same boarding house. You lead your brother astray, Santiago. You are to have no communication with him."

"But Papa . . ." Pedro protested. However, before my father's stern glance, he fell silent immediately.

"For the time remaining," my father instructed me, "you will devote yourself to studying. Perhaps in some way," he added drily, "your mind will thus be prepared for the tasks ahead."

"Yes, of course, Papa," I said submissively. I had expected much worse after my "affair of the rose" had been revealed to my father. To be sent to Huesca to school would perhaps not be too bad, and Pedro would be there. Not for a moment could I imagine that Pedro and I would live in the same city and not see one another. The studying, it seemed, was to begin at once. Obediently I went to my room where my father piled books upon the bed. Putting his hand firmly upon one text, he ordered, "You will begin by reviewing the Latin you have learned, if you have learned any Latin at all." I stared sullenly at the book. "How foolish and headstrong you are," my father said suddenly. "Do you realize what an opportunity is being given you? When I think how I struggled to receive an education . . ." He made an impatient gesture with his hand and left the room.

I pushed the books to one side and flung myself down upon the bed. If only my father would not persist in trying to make a scholar of me. I would never be a doctor, never! I would be an artist or I would be nothing! But how to draw here, in my room, where at any moment I might be discovered? There was no lock upon the door; even if there were, I would not dare use it, for instantly I would be suspected of some wrongdoing. No. I must create for myself a little world of my own to which I could retire and draw to my heart's ease. I stared up at the ceiling of my room. At first I could think of nothing; then, suddenly, I remembered the pigeon house. The pigeon house was little more than a room attached to the barn which had fallen into disuse. Smiling to myself, I opened my Latin book. I even glanced at one or two of the pages. Anyone peering in would see Santiago devoting himself to his studies; actually my mind was racing with possibilities for using the pigeon house.

I waited a few days before broaching the subject. When we were at the table waiting dinner, I said, "Latin requires much concentration. Do you agree, Papa?"

He looked up from his food. "Then I suggest that you concentrate."

"I would do so gladly, Papa, except that there are so many distractions."

He put down his knife and fork.

"What distractions?"

"Pedro comes in and out." I hoped Pedro would forgive me for using him this way. "It is, after all, Papa, as much his room as mine. There is the clatter of the pots and pans, the voices of those who come to see you, Papa. I cannot keep my mind from straying from my books."

"And what do you suggest?" my father asked. "That I turn my study over to you?"

"Most certainly not!" I was truly shocked. Never would I wish such a thing. "I thought perhaps the pigeon house. It is quiet there, and I would be undisturbed . . ."

My father gave me a long, hard look. "I would like to believe, Santiago," he said finally, "that you have come to your senses and are prepared to study." Clearly he doubted this, but my mother, sweet, good person that she is, believed my every word. I wished she did not, for it upset me to be forced to lie to her.

But what other way could I achieve the privacy I so desperately sought?

"Can I help you fix up the pigeon house?" Pedro asked, when my father consented.

"You are not angry with me, Pedro?"

"Angry? Why should I be angry? You are not like me, Santiago. You need to be alone. Would you not respect this need if it were mine?"

Is there another one such as Pedro? I think not. He helped me bring a small table and chair to the pigeon house, and set about industriously to clean it, as well, for there was dust everywhere in the room. Me, I am not so meticulous, but Pedro has an orderly soul.

"Look, Santiago. The window overlooks the Cuideras's garret and roof. I wonder what he keeps up there."

I went to the window to stand beside Pedro. "Since he runs the confectionary store, I imagine he keeps extra supplies in the garret," I commented idly. At the moment, the house of Señor Roberto Cuideras was of little interest to me. However, the proximity of the roof gave me an additional idea.

"Pedro," I said, "do you wish to help me further?" He waited expectantly. "Do you think you can bring me some brushwood and sticks? . . ."

"What kind of sticks?"

"Sticks! What do I care what kind? An assortment. Big. Little."

While Pedro was gone, I went into the barn and found some boards which I brought back to the pigeon house. One board I laid across from the windowsill to the roof of Señor Cuideras's house; then, proceeding with caution, I walked along my improvised bridge, carrying another of the boards. When Pedro returned, I would not permit him to use the bridge; instead, he stood at the window and handed me the brushwood and sticks he had collected, and watched wide-eyed as I constructed a crude hideaway on the Cuideras's roof.

"What do you plan to do now?" Pedro asked when at last I returned through the window.

"It will be my painting room," I replied grandly. Pedro was filled with admiration for my ingenuity.

"Papa will never find you out there," he said. For a long moment, I felt the qualms of conscience. My father was right; I was a bad influence upon my brother. But my need was greater than my conscience, so Pedro helped me sneak my drawing supplies — the paper, the pencils, the paints and brushes — to the pigeon room, whence I carefully carted them to my hideaway on the Cuideras's roof. I was not visible from below, but I was able to keep careful watch on my own house. Whenever I saw anyone approaching — my father came on surprise visits to see if I really studied; my mother occasionally brought small snacks in her effort to restore weight to my body — I walked back across the plank to the pigeon house and pulled the plank in hastily.

I could not keep my friends from visiting me in the pigeon house, and once they discovered my lean-to on the adjoining roof, they came to inspect that, as well, promising all the while to respect my privacy the moment I indicated I wished to be alone. It was the morning Francisco ran surely along the plank that I made my great discovery. Francisco was restless. He moved about on the roof carelessly, and was at times quite visible from below. To entice him away from view, I suggested that we peer into the garret window and see what treasures Señor Cuideras had stored in the attic.

I rubbed my sleeve against the window and pressed my face against it. And drew in my breath sharply. *"Qué bello!"* Francisco pushed me aside, took stock of what Señor Cuideras stored in his garret, turned to me, grinning, and agreed, "You are right, Santiago. It is a beautiful sight, is it not?"

How strange! We are both of the same age; we have eyes to see, and we looked into the same space. Yet I saw only the books piled high on old pieces of furniture while Francisco could hardly tear his gaze from box after box of sweetmeats and dried fruits. He danced about me in glee. "I will tell Lope and the others. You are a genius, Santiago! Now we will not raid the orchards for a while. We will visit Señor Cuideras's garret instead."

"No!"

Francisco gaped, open-mouthed.

"That is stealing, Francisco. I do not steal."

His face flushed. "And what was the small matter of risking our very lives to get for you roses from the gardens of the marquis?" he demanded indignantly. "And what of the fruit we have taken from the trees in

93

the orchards? By what fancy name do you call such things, eh, Santiago?"

"Flowers and fruit that grow in God's clean air are for all. But these things you see, these are Señor Cuideras's stock, from which he makes a living. Do you understand, Francisco?"

"No, I do not comprehend such fine distinctions," Francisco said, aggrieved. "To take what does not belong to one is stealing, whether it is a flower in a garden, an apple from an orchard, or those tantalizing confections in the garret."

Of course, Francisco was right, yet this feeling within me would not permit me to take from Señor Cuideras one piece of candy or fruit. Rather than try to explain further, I tried to persuade Francisco another way. "I tell you what I will do, Francisco. Bring the others and I will read to you, one by one, the books of Señor Cuideras."

"That is hardly the same thing," Francisco replied hotly, but since I remained firm, he had little choice. "Very well," he said finally, yielding ungraciously. "I will go and get Claudio, Juan, and the others."

Francisco has a most generous nature; once he accepted my stand, he made no further reference to the treasure of confections in the garret. Instead he and the others listened raptly as I read, one by one, such books as *The Three Musketeers* by the elder Dumas, *The Hunchback of Notre Dame* by Victor Hugo, and our favorite of all, Defoe's *Robinson Crusoe*. Each morning they appeared in the pigeon house, crossed the plank, and settled themselves behind the chimney on the

Cuideras's roof, Pedro among them, for I could no longer deny him the right to walk on the board that bridged the space. So absorbed were we in the reading that once or twice we were almost caught. Fortunately, Pedro remained alert and signaled me. I fled back to the pigeon house and opened my Latin grammar, giving the appearance of one lost in studies as my father poked his head into the room. He saw me with the book open, my head bent over it, yet doubt nagged him.

"It is a remarkable change that has come over you, Santiago," he remarked cynically. "Perhaps I should return you to the Esculapian fathers. They seem to have taught you the value of applying yourself to your studies." When I began to voice a loud protest, he merely lifted his hand for silence. "Have no fear. You are going to Huesca." He ran his hand thoughtfully across his chin. When he left me at last, I could see that he still felt much unease.

So the days passed. When my friends came, I read to them; when they left, I sat peacefully in my lean-to and drew whatever came to my mind. However, I, too, grew restless and once again sought some more physical activity. Accordingly, one morning Pedro and I left the house quite early — my father was away on a call to the village of Linás — and met José and the others in the public square.

"No reading today?" Claudio asked.

I pointed to the mountain peak. "Today we do not read. Today we act. To the castle!" I cried. We ran willingly from the square, eager to climb to the ruins and there play out our games of knights in feudal battle. As usual, I directed our action, for my memory for the things I read in books is more to be relied upon than the others'. They charged about in most satisfactory fashion until the heat of the day penetrated even the ruins. We abandoned the castle to move on to the nearby *sarda*, a forest of live oaks whose beginnings, I do not doubt, go back to antiquity. Here we became mighty hunters, passing the time shooting at birds with our bows and arrows. Fortunately for the birds, they were fleeter in the air than the arrows we loosed at them. Claudio, Francisco, Lope, and the others persisted; I soon lost interest and, leaving them behind, went searching for the nests of magpies.

I could hear the cries of my friends for some little while; later the silence of the woods closed me in. I walked along, climbing higher, until I emerged from the forest. Looking up at the sky, I saw an eagle wheeling away from the peak of a tremendous cliff. Have I not told you before that I collected both birds' eggs and nestlings? This is the truth; I had nurtured many species. But never an eaglet! I had never even seen the nest of an eagle; I had never viewed close up an eagle's egg or its young born. I forgot all about my brother and my friends; now I could think only that I must climb somehow to the top of that cliff to see the nest of this majestic bird. I think perhaps that day I had in me the heart and blood of a mountain goat, for without any equipment save a small clasp-knife which I carried always, I scaled a series of ledges. My clothing ripped; my skin was scraped from my knees and my hands, but I have a great persistence within me that is not easily turned aside. At last I came within sight of the nest and could almost have touched it. I knew that such a bird must of course build for itself a large home; that it would be of so great a size was almost unbelievable. And so cunningly constructed! How I wish I could have watched this giant bird place in position the sticks of the nest and line it with grass and leaves. Some eagles, I have read, even use bits of wool and fur as lining.

There were two eaglets in the nest. From their appearance, I judged that they would soon be ready to fly. As you know, the young birds cannot fly during the first eleven to sixteen weeks of their lives. My father says that I act on impulse and do not stop to think out the consequences of my actions. In this respect, my father knows me well, for certainly what happened next I brought upon myself. So anxious was I to study the eaglets, I forgot the mother bird swooping across the golden sky. She came plummeting down, her wings widespread, her eyes glittering, her long, razor-sharp talons at the ready. She would have torn me to bits to protect her young. I could feel my heart turn over in my chest. Without thinking, other than that I needed to leave this spot at once, I leaped to a ledge below. There was a small hollow area at the back of the ledge. I crept into it, folding my body into as little a space as was possible, huddling there while the enraged bird tried again and again to dislodge me. Never shall I forget her cries, nor the rushing sound of her wings as she charged the ledge. Whether she tired

of the attack or now considered the eaglets safe, I do not know, only that when she flew away finally, I was able to breathe freely once more.

My whole body trembled; I was glad there was no one to see how I lay upon the ledge, shaking, my face and the palms of my hands damp with perspiration. I could not move — and swore to myself that I did not wish to move — from that spot, but after a while I began to think about getting back to the *sarda*, or to the castle ruins, or better still, home.

I looked about me carefully, assessing my problem. And what a problem I had presented myself by leaping to this ledge. I could not ascend even if I wished to: on the one hand, the eagle was vigilant; on the other, I saw that I stood facing a wall so high and so smooth I could not climb it. Beneath the ledge upon which I stood was a series of other ledges, but one so far from the other that to jump down was impossible. I crawled back to the hollow and stared miserably into space. What was I to do now? What madness had prompted me to leave my sanctuary on Señor Cuideras's roof to come here? I will die here on this ledge, I thought, and who will know? When I do not return home, my father and mother will believe I ran away, as so often I had threatened; Pedro and my friends will believe this also. No! They would think I was still in the *sarda* and that I had become lost.

I would not even have a funeral. I would simply disappear and, after some time had passed, I would be forgotten. I was filled with much pity for myself, there on my lonely ledge. Never before had the hours gone by so slowly. The sun burned its way from overhead toward its western goal, and from its leisurely path across the sky I could tell how long I had been marooned on this mountain. I was too anxious to be hungry, but my lips and throat begged for water. I rose from the hollow and stared up and then down, as I had done so many times I had lost count. Always the smoothness defeated me. If only I had a rope or a ladder! A ladder! Had I not created a ladder when I needed to escape from the locked classroom in the school of the Esculapian fathers? Could I not be equally ingenious now? I searched my pockets for my clasp-knife. Edging clear of the side where the eagle's nest lay, I inched my way along the ledge, which extended narrowly some fifteen feet farther on. Using my knife, I began to dig into a shallow crack about knee height, and into another about shoulder height. Fortunately for both the knife and my energy, the rock was relatively soft. I tested the enlarged cracks. They gave me just enough hold for my hands and feet. I almost shouted, but remembered the eagle. I had seen her leave, to go foraging for food for her young ones, no doubt, but I did not wish to draw attention to myself any more than I could help. Slowly, every few feet, I dug into the surface of the rock. Once I looked down and grew somewhat dizzy; I took care not to do this again. Another time I thought I heard the eagle behind me and froze against the mountainside, my heart thudding, my fingers gripping the crevice until the knuckles showed white. Yet I persisted, step after long, hard step. When I reached the top, I threw myself down and gave thanks to my patron saint, who had surely watched over me during this period of trial. I rested a few moments. However, in spite of my weariness, I was anxious to get home. I followed a path — an animal path, rugged, difficult, but at least a path upon which I could remain upright and moving!

When I reached the *sarda*, Pedro and the others, naturally, were no longer there, nor were they playing among the ruins of the castle. I went now more quickly down the mountain, for here the path was larger and easier and I knew it well. When I reached the public square, I could have kissed each cobblestone with joy. I ran home. My mother came to the door when I entered, scized me with a quick embrace while she scolded, "Where have you been, Santiago? How could you frighten us this way?" and in the same breath added, "Your father waits for you. In the pigeon house."

"I thought Papa went to Linás . . ."

"He went and he returned."

Reluctantly she released me; equally reluctantly I forced myself to go to the pigeon house. I climbed up, my feet dragging more on this ladder than the one I had dug into the side of the mountain, to find my father sitting quietly at the table, the Latin text open in his hands. My eyes flew to the window; evidently Pedro or Francisco or Lope or one of the others had come to the pigeon house while I clung to my ledge and had walked across to Señor Cuideras's roof, for the edge of the plank showed clearly across the windowsill.

"You will take down the shed you have built on

Señor Cuideras's roof," my father said impassively, "and you will not use the pigeon house again."

I nodded. That this would happen I had expected.

My father picked up the whip which lay across the table. This, too, I had expected.

When he was done beating me, I said bitterly, "Tell me, Papa. Do you enjoy this?" I thought he would lift the whip and use it again, but instead he flung it from him into a corner of the room, looked at me steadily with an expression I could not fathom, and left the room without a word.

ELEVEN

For the rest of the summer, I tried, I tell you this truly, to avoid mischief, although the temptation was always there. Whether I succeeded I do not know, for what appeared to me to be but normal activity did not strike my father in the same light. I was almost glad when the time came for me to go to school again, this time in Huesca. Pedro did not go with me, my father having decided that Pedro was not yet ready to leave home, so I had not even the hope of his companionship. In Huesca there was no Uncle Juan, no Timoteo, not even the gnarled and crotchety Estrellita of the mean look and the good but grudging heart. Instead I was installed in a boarding house which was inhabited, for the most part, by young men studying for the priesthood. Such an atmosphere, my father firmly believed, would surely have some effect upon me.

A Señora Margarita Arco owned the boarding house. She was a severe woman, her hair pulled back to form a rigid bun on the back of her head, her eyes black and unsmiling, her lips thin and clamped together. Perhaps she was not inwardly so; she fed me well and kept my room immaculate, no easy task, I am the first to admit. My concern, however, was not for the house where I lived. My more immediate problem, as usual, was my life at school.

The first moment I stepped foot in the courtyard of the Institute, I was immediately surrounded by a group of boys. Outstanding among them was a big coarse fellow, a real *perro de presa*, a bulldog of a figure, with a brutish expression. His name, I learned soon enough, was Azcón, and he came from Alcalá de Gállego, sent by the devil himself to plague me. I was not surprised to find myself so encircled. It is only to be expected when you are a new boy. Is it not the way of the world, that new boys are fair game for bullies?

"You, there!" Azcón said. "Where are you from?"

"I am from Ayerbe," I returned politely. "My name is Santiago Ramón y Cajal."

"Santiago Ramón y Cajal," he mimicked me. Immediately the other boys laughed. A bully is a great wit to his followers. "Your name is Goatflesh," Azcón said flatly. "Repeat after me, 'My name is Goatflesh.' "

"Goatflesh! Goatflesh!" the others chanted.

Now, surrounded as I was, I should sensibly have agreed. After all, it was only a name. And I was one against many. But I have this unfortunate stubbornness. So instead I smiled pleasantly and told him to go to the devil. Perhaps I did not put it quite so courteously. In any case, his eyes opened wide, for who would expect a new boy, one alone, to be so foolhardy?

"Oho! This one wishes to be a hero," he told his cronies. "Let us show Goatflesh how we deal with heroes."

The object of a battle is to take the enemy by surprise, usually an advantage. Before Azcón moved, I leaped at him, landing a satisfying fist upon his nose and drawing first blood. Then, while he still stood amazed, I whirled about, giving one boy a black eye and another a telling midriff blow, before they all closed in upon me. I have had my share of beatings — from my father, from my teachers, from other students — but never one to equal the punishment now inflicted upon me. I defended myself as best I could, but before long I was rolling on the ground, intent only upon protecting my body from the vicious kicks and my head from the pummeling fists. Suddenly their shouting ceased. All grew quiet. I lay a few moments without moving, my eyes closed. A voice said, "They are gone. Can you get up?"

I looked up. A tall man with unruly, blond hair, his brows almost invisible over lively, chestnut brown eyes, his mustache as fair as the hair on his head, bristling and full, was standing over me. I rose to my feet, painfully.

"Thank you," I said through swelling lips.

"Welcome to the Institute of Huesca," he said sardonically. "I am Don Carlos Ventura. I teach geography." He put his hand under my elbow to steady me. "Would you prefer to go home and rest . . . I do not know your name . . ."

"Santiago Ramón y Cajal."

". . . Santiago, or do you wish to begin classes today?"

"I will attend classes." I began to brush at my clothing.

"Where are you from, Santiago?"

"Ayerbe."

"So," he whistled, drawing out the word. "And they called you Goatflesh." He regarded me with a keen look. "It was nothing personal, you know, Santiago. All boys who come from Ayerbe are called Goatflesh. They accept it, and soon our bullies grow tired of the game."

I wiped blood from my nose with the back of my hand.

"I will not accept it," I said stubbornly. "They will call me Santiago."

Thus did my school days begin. Except for Azcón and those who followed him, it was not too bad. True, I still had Latin classes, but my teacher was a gentle old man, somewhat deaf and not a little blind. It is hard to believe that two men so different, Don Antonio and Father Jacinto, can live in the same world. Both tried to teach Latin, Father Jacinto through terror, Don Antonio through kindliness, and neither succeeded. For the one drove every rational thought from one's head and the other simply could not control his students. Boys can be devils; I tell you this from my heart. Don Antonio deserved better, but the young can be very cruel to the aged, is it not so?

The subject I enjoyed most was geography. In Don Carlos's class, there was discipline. He was strong enough to impose it; further, any horseplay and the offending student was immediately and bodily ejected from the room. In addition, Don Carlos kept a record. Every note against a name could mean the difference between failing and passing. In this class, we were forever drawing maps. There was much grumbling among the students. Islands and continents assumed strange shapes as the pupils applied themselves. Rivers ran peculiar courses, and mountains struggled upward on paper in impossible ranges.

But I enjoyed it. How I enjoyed it! That and my wanderings through Huesca were my only pleasures in life. So small a thing to lift the heart, this meandering through the different areas of Huesca, you may think. But do you know what it means to someone from a small village to roam city streets? Real streets, not dusty roads which are little more than enlarged animal paths? I could not get my fill of city sights. The first time I made my way to the cathedral, I stood open-mouthed before it. Never had I seen such a doorway. It had seven arches, each arch slightly larger than the one next to it. Sculpted on the door, apostles, martyrs, and saints stood forth boldly. Whether the art was good or bad, I could not judge; I knew only that it sent shivers of excitement through me. Our church in Ayerbe had small, stained-glass windows, but here, in the cathedral, the rose window was incredibly large. Inside, the cathedral was equally impressive, particularly the altarpiece, which was made of alabaster, that beautiful translucent mineral with its pearly luster and its smoothly polished surface.

I went also to the oldest of churches in Huesca, the church of San Pedro el Viejo. What history was there! The cathedral soared, but San Pedro el Viejo was a study in gloom, damp, depressing, a relic of the time when the Mozárabes, who were Christian Moors, were still powerful in Spain. Fascinated, I visited the tombs, where the once-great rulers and princes of Aragón were buried. As I was standing there, straining my eyes to read what was engraved in the stone, a voice spoke almost in my ear. I jumped. Turning, I saw a young man, one I had seen coming and going in the boarding house, always with an air of remoteness.

"I see that you are studying the tomb of the monk-king. You are interested in his life?"

"I do not even know who he is," I confessed candidly.

"He was Ramiro the Second, King of Aragón in the twelfth century."

"And he was called the monk-king because he was made loving and kind by religion?" I guessed.

The young man stared at me steadily. "In the year 1136, Ramiro summoned to his side certain nobles who had shown a spirit of rebellion against their king. 'I will cast a bell,' he told them, when they had assembled, 'a bell whose message shall ring throughout the kingdom, a bell so unusual it shall be remembered as long as time exists. Would you wish to see such a bell being cast?' he asked them."

"How beautiful," I interrupted. "To cast a bell to be remembered as long as time exists."

The young man blinked his eyes, but otherwise disregarded my interruption. I could only assume that perhaps he worked here as a guide at times, and did not tolerate well anyone breaking the thread of his story.

"The nobles crowded round him eagerly," the young man continued. "They did not trust Ramiro. Nonetheless, they were anxious to witness the making of so remarkable a bell."

"Is this where the bell was cast?" I wondered.

"Here? But of course not," he replied impatiently. "It happened in the royal Alcazar, the palace, which is the same building that houses the Institute."

"The school? My school?"

"When next you have time, visit the dungeon. It is reached by a flight of narrow steps made of stone which go down . . ."

"I have no wish to visit a dungeon. Prisons hold no fascination for me."

"Do you wish to hear this story? Then be quiet and listen. There is more to come. Now then. To witness this great occurrence, the nobles were instructed that they must enter the chamber, one by one, when summoned. To this also the nobles agreed. Thus, one by one, they descended the stone stairway; one by one, the king slew them. He beheaded them, placing their heads carefully to form a circle on the floor of the dungeon. When he was finished, there lacked but one thing in this monstrous human bell — the clapper. Therefore, he summoned the bishop, Ordás, and with his head was the bell completed."

I shuddered. His matter-of-fact tone, coupled with the aura of the tombs, chilled me. "If you will excuse me," I muttered. He shrugged, and I fled gladly into the sunshine and made my way to the Isuela, a small stream surrounded by parklike groves, where the songs of the birds and the beauty of butterflies in flight restored my tranquillity of soul.

Each day followed a pattern. In the morning I left the boarding house, went to school, was beaten by Azcón and his faithful followers, learned as little as possible, dragged myself back to the boarding house ragged, dirty, and bloody, or skipped classes when I wished to be by myself.

One morning Don Carlos requested me to remain a few moments after class. The other students exchanged smirks. How wonderful when someone else is the object of a teacher's wrath! But I had done nothing wrong, if you can believe this. Apprehensive, I waited until the room was empty. Don Carlos turned to me and said abruptly, "You have great talent, Santiago. Do you know this?"

I gawked at him. "For geography?" I asked, amazed.

"Geography? No, no. I speak now of your drawing ability. What is your goal in life, Santiago? Have you given thought to your future?"

"My father is a doctor. He wishes me also to study medicine."

Don Carlos worried his mustache, a habit many men have, this business of caressing the hair on the upper lip, stroking it endlessly with forefinger and thumb. "I did not ask you what your father wishes. I asked what you wish."

"I have only one desire, but my father will never allow it."

"And that is?"

"To study art."

His eyes grew brighter. "Splendid, Santiago. Tell me, does your father know of your talent?"

"He does not consider it such." Quickly I explained the incident with the painter of our church walls and his momentous decision that had shipped me off to Jaca and the Esculapian friars. "So you see," I concluded, "why my father will not hear of it."

"A house painter! I cannot believe it! Your father is an educated man. You must have misunderstood him." His fingers rapped energetically upon his desk. "I will write to your father. I will urge him to let you matriculate in art. Have no fear, Santiago. I will persuade him."

My throat was so tight with emotion I could not utter a single word in gratitude. I backed from the room until I reached the door, flung it open, and ran down the corridor. My face must have grown pale with excitement, for at the end of the corridor Azcón stopped me.

"Hey, Goatflesh! Have you seen a ghost? What did

111

Don Carlos want with you? Has he thrown you out of class?" The questions came rapidly, one after the other. I tried to push Azcón aside. He seized my arm and squeezed it. "I asked you a question, Goatflesh."

"You asked me many questions."

"All right. Many questions. Now I wish an answer."

"The answer is . . ."

"Yes?" he asked eagerly.

"None of your business."

He dug his hand deeper into my arm. "I shall twist it from your socket, Goatflesh," he said pleasantly. At that moment, one of the instructors came out of a classroom and approached us. Azcón dropped his hand and moved off. But he would not forget. Like a bulldog, he was tenacious, particularly since two months had now passed from the day I had come to school and I had still not knuckled under to him.

While the weather was still warm, I had been working on a grand plan to overcome Azcón, for I believed that if I could beat him, the others would leave me alone, as well. Each day, whenever I had sufficient time, I hurried off to the wooded areas along the banks of the Isuela. There, where none could see me, I performed like an athlete in training. I hung from branches, pulling myself up and down; I climbed trees to acquire agility; I tugged at stones, the heavier the better, and lifted them as far as I could over my head to gain muscle. I ran and jumped and somersaulted. Thanks to my tormentor, I was daily gaining in good health!

Thus the weeks slipped by. Each day I faced two hopes — to conquer Azcón, and to learn good news from Ayerbe. Whenever I walked into geography class, I gave Don Carlos a questioning glance. Time after time he shook his head. At last Don Carlos called me aside.

"Your father is a busy man, of that I have no doubt," Don Carlos said brusquely, "but surely common courtesy would suggest to him that he reply to my letter concerning his son."

"My father is not an ordinary man," I admitted. "If he is not pleased — and I am sure he is not pleased — then he will disregard the matter. Besides, I am sure he does not consider this of much importance."

"Not important?" Don Carlos was shocked. "His son's future not important?"

"No, no," I said. "The future is most important, but only how he plans it, Don Carlos. He is not a man to change his mind easily. My father," I added thoughtfully, "is a stubborn man."

"I am also stubborn," Don Carlos said angrily. "I will write him again."

I had come to the Institute at Huesca toward the end of September. The days seemed to move with leaden slowness, but even so somehow time fled, and now it was December. The weather had turned cold; I shivered in my jacket; my face and fingers burned where they were nipped by frost. One morning Señora Arco confronted me. In her hands she held a winter coat.

"Today you will not leave for school until you put

on your coat," she commanded. "I will not have you get sick because you neglect yourself, and have your father lay the blame upon me."

I stared at the coat. I thought I had hidden it well in my closet, but evidently not so cleverly as I had imagined.

"I am not cold, Señora," I insisted. "This weather — it is only brisk. I am used to much colder days than this."

She barred my way. "You will not leave this house without your coat."

I am convinced that women of good heart will yet bring the world to its knees! My mother, whom I love, had fashioned the coat for me, cutting down an old coat that had belonged to my father. I am tall, but my father is taller still. My mother reasons that I will grow, perhaps even to tower over my father one day. Therefore, what does one do? One observes economy. The coat does not fit the boy but soon the boy may fit the coat. The garment was warm; it was serviceable; it was hideous — and I would rather have died than put it on. So I put it on, for though I am stubborn, I cannot defeat the will of such women as my mother and Señora Arco.

Azcón and his followers had lost some interest in me — not altogether, you understand, but enough to make life passable. Now, when I walked into the schoolyard, my coat slapping ludicrously at my calves, Azcón and the others lined up about me and stared in disbelief.

"Look at our Goatflesh!" Azcón cried. "He has turned into an organ grinder!"

"Hey, organ grinder," another called. "Where is your monkey?"

"Don't forget the organ. He needs an organ as well as the monkey."

I sprang at Azcón, knocking him down. My days in the groves had indeed improved my fighting prowess. But I was outnumbered by his friends and inconvenienced by the coat. I fell before them and was rescued only by the call to class.

When school was over and I returned to the boarding house, I moved quietly up the steps, hoping to escape Señora Arco's sharp scrutiny. A foolish hope, for she met me at the top of the stairway, where she stood holding fresh linens in her arms. I expected her to scold, for the coat my mother had labored to make was torn and filthy. Instead, she said, surprisingly, "Santiago, you are a clever boy. Why do you not fight with your head instead of your fists?"

"All this would not have happened if you had not insisted I wear this accursed coat," I said coldly. "Or if my mother had only made the coat to fit. For a few inches of cloth, regard what has happened to me."

"Nonsense," she replied tranquilly. "It would not matter to them if you were clothed in the latest of fashions. It is you they wish to subdue. You must either submit or conquer. All new boys suffer this fate. I have sons. I know."

"I will not submit. And I am trying to conquer," I told her, "but I do not know how."

"You will think of a way," she said again. "Now be so kind as to give me the coat. I will repair it for you."

Seeing my face fall, she added kindly, "and I will shorten it, Santiago."

"You are a blessed angel, Señora," I said fervently.

"I am a mother of sons," she said drily. Taking my coat, she moved past me down the steps.

TWELVE

I DO NOT SEEK TROUBLE. I tell you this honestly.
But have you not observed how trouble sometimes
seems to search one out, as if fate says: This is the one.
That morning in January, for example. The weather
had turned much colder, freezing, in fact. What more
simple than the idea of going ice-skating on the mill
pond? Do you not agree? Is not ice-skating a quiet,
enjoyable, pleasant sport? It was a Saturday morning;
my attendance was not required in school. Therefore I
made my way to the mill pond early, hoping I would
have it to myself. When I approached, I was happy to
see that the pond was frozen solid and that it was
deserted. In moments I was skimming across the ice.
As you may perhaps suspect, however, my solitude
lasted briefly. Soon I heard the sound of voices calling
and much laughter. My heart turned over. You do
not believe such a thing may happen? It does. The
heart flips in the body; one can feel it.

"Look who is here. The organ grinder," a familiar
voice shouted.

"Hey, Goatflesh," another called.

I pretended not to hear.

"What? We cannot get his attention?" Azcón said mockingly. "I think I know how to do this." With that, he picked up a large stone and hurled it at the ice near where I skated. Instantly the others seized upon this notion gleefully. Stone after stone came hurtling down on the ice. Before long, a hole appeared, a large gaping hole. Azcón and his followers skated close to me, once again imprisoning me in a loose semicircle. I attempted to skate away, but whichever direction I turned, they blocked my passage.

"You do not like our company?" Azcón asked, pretending to be hurt. "We have no wish to keep you here. Why don't you leave, eh, Goatflesh?"

I stood still, wondering what action I might take. I did not wish to remain on the pond any longer; the day had already been spoiled for me. On the other hand, I did not relish the idea of another fight and another beating. There was only one course for me to pursue. I skated back a short way, then, picking up speed, raced toward the hole and leaped across. I landed on the other side well enough. Unfortunately, however, the ice there had been somewhat loosened by the rocks and the dark green water which had consequently welled up. It sagged beneath my weight. There was a crunching noise, the ice broke off, and I fell into the arctic water, sinking like a boulder. Terrified, I thrashed about wildly, trying to reach the surface again. I moved up and discovered solid ice above me! I could not find the opening! I would have

prayed if I had had the breath and if I were not paralyzed with fear.

"I cannot breathe! I cannot breathe!" These words were repeated in my mind like a litany. But I would not give up. I bobbed up again and again, my hands searching futilely until at last in their fumbling they touched open space. I pulled myself up, grasping the ice rimming the edge of the hole, and took a deep breath. "Help me! Help me!" I cried. Surely even Azcón and the others would not leave me behind to drown. I looked about. They were gone; once again I had the mill pond entirely to myself. They had fled in terror, fearing that I had indeed drowned and they would be called to account. What was I to do? I could not get a grip upon the ice though I tried over and over. I struggled, my teeth chattering, my body shivering, clutching at the slippery, frozen rim and kicking out desperately to remain afloat. Suddenly my foot touched a stake. Using it as a lever, I hurled myself forward. Gasping and groaning, I worried my tired body inch by inch out of the water and onto the solid polar surface. I wanted nothing more than to lie face down upon that frozen area, to rest, even to sleep. Get up, Santiago, a voice within me whispered. Get up. To lie here is death. You must move. Slowly I rose and made my way across the ice and back to the land. I was wet clear through; the bitter north wind blew without mercy. My clothing began to freeze and to become stiff, making walking almost impossible.

What solution to this problem? The mill! I would take refuge inside the mill until my clothing was dry. I went as hastily as I could toward this sanctuary, but when I got there, the door would not open. I pounded upon the door, hoping the farmer might be within, but it was hopeless. Now what was I to do? I do not justify what I did next; perhaps another might have reached some other conclusion, although I am not so sure. After all, I had survived a somewhat harrowing experience. I was thoroughly chilled. I could almost hear each individual bone in my body shivering one against the other. I moved around the mill out of the biting north wind to the east to face the cheerless winter sun. There I took off all my clothes, wrung them out as best I could, and spread them carefully upon the ground. To keep warm, I began to run around and around the mill. When I had exercised in the woods, building my strength and endurance for a final contest with Azcón, I never dreamed that those same exercises would be so helpful to me in another, more drastic, situation. How ironic is our fate!

In any case, I was intent only upon the necessity of keeping warm. That my action might seem exceedingly strange to anyone never crossed my mind until a loud, angry voice shouted at me, *"Indecente! Obsceno!"* It was the farmer approaching me, waving his fist in the air.

"Señor, if you will permit me to explain," I began, but he broke in harshly. "Do you think you can come among decent folk . . . *obsceno!*" he sputtered.

"Hey, Santiago," someone called. When I turned, I saw a boy from the school standing there, grinning at me. *"Qué pasa?"*

"Nothing," I snapped.

"You know him?" the farmer asked the boy, jerking his thumb in my direction.

"Sure. That's Santiago Ramón y Cajal. He is a student at the Institute."

"He is *loco*," the farmer said.

It was getting to be too much. I had been tormented, almost drowned, frozen, frightened, called crazy, indecent, and obscene. And standing here naked, I was beginning to turn blue. Without another word, I picked up my clothes and put them on. They were still quite damp, but much better than before.

"I am sorry if I have offended you, Señor," I tried one last time, but he would not listen.

"The director of the school shall hear from me," he threatened. "What are you all doing on the mill pond anyway?" he exploded, turning to shout at some boys and girls who were now gathering on the ice. "Have you no respect for private property?"

"We will do nothing more than skate," one of the girls from the town said nicely.

"Yes," a boy added. "We are not all like Santiago."

Grumbling, the mill owner at last agreed to permit the girls from the town and the boys from the Institute to continue to skate. As for me, there was nothing more I waited to hear. Once my clothes were on, I headed for home as quickly as I could.

No one was about when I arrived at the boarding house, except for the young man whom I had met at the Church of San Pedro el Viejo. He was just coming down the steps, a Bible tucked under his arm. He gave me a brief nod and continued on his way without a word. I stared after him. My thoughts on my return from the mill had centered upon Azcón. I had built satisfying pictures in my mind, visions of myself fighting him and conquering, with Azcón on the ground and me astride his prone body, administering the punishment that had been mine all these long months. Now I was struck with an idea so simple, so magnificent, I could not understand why it had never occurred to me before. Señora Arco was right. Why had I not used my head in all this time? The Bible would guide me. I went up the steps, three at a time, and collapsed upon my bed. I stared at the ceiling, smiling broadly. Oh what a surprise was in store for Azcón!

THIRTEEN

Do you not sometimes look back at your life and think how different it might have been if only you had done this or not done that, if this event had not occurred, or that one, if this person had spoken to you kindly or that person had acted another way? Would I still be the same Santiago Ramón y Cajal if my father had loved me? If he had taken me in his arms when I was four and led me gently to learning instead of to the cave and the lessons in that fearful, shadowy place? I suppose it is useless to look back and wonder, for there is no returning, no changing what has happened.

What took place at school in the next months, from January to May, was of my own doing. I do not deny this. Yet perhaps even these events occurred because a child of four was lost and unloved. Or do you think, like my father and some of the schoolmasters — Father Jacinto, for example — that I was simply a donkey, obstinate, slow, willful, stupid? The burro, as you well know, when he makes up his mind he is abused, will dig his heels into the ground and refuse to go either forward or backward, no matter how many blows are rained upon his back. But even this dull-witted creature can be led if a carrot is dangled before his nose. No matter. Let us speak of other things now. Let us talk of the rest of my school year, which began in triumph and ended, as always, in disaster.

Do you recall my mentioning a surprise for Azcón? It was so simple a solution to my problem I could not understand why I had been so long in finding it. However, when emotion rules the mind, reason becomes clouded. At any rate, I was thinking clearly now.

When I had seen the Bible in the hands of the young man studying for the priesthood, suddenly there came to me the story of David and Goliath. David knew the true value of the sling. Could I not profit from his example? My hand, I can assure you, had lost none of its cunning since I had come to Huesca. I could still shoot, with deadly accuracy, four or five stones in the time that others were still fitting one pebble into position.

My friends Lope and Francisco and Juan and the others and I had made good use of our slings in Ayerbe. The time had come for me to do likewise in Huesca. Having carefully examined the sling I had brought with me from home, I decided it was not good enough and therefore I set about constructing a new one, obtaining silk from Señora Arco to use for the cords and leather from a local cobbler for the strap. The rest of that day I spent hunting for stones. This is an important task, for the pebbles I use must be spherical in shape, heavy to the touch and smooth, and of a size to fit the sling snugly.

When the following Monday arrived, my plan of action was well mapped in my mind. I went to the Institute long before the other students so that I had time, in the quiet of the schoolyard, to line up a series of bottles on a wall. I brought with me as well a hat which I jammed down upon my head. When all was in readiness, I waited patiently until the schoolyard began to fill with students, among them, of course, Azcón and his crew. When he caught sight of me, he stopped short.

"So! You are not dead, Goatflesh," he said. Whether he was relieved or sorry, I could not tell.

"My name is Santiago Ramón y Cajal," I replied calmly, "and soon you will repeat it after me." Without waiting for a reply, I reached into my sack of stones and let fly. The stone flew past his ear, so close it sang like a bee in its search for nectar.

"Hey!" Azcón said, startled. "You almost hit me in the head."

I sent another stone sailing past him, this time on the other side. "Almost because I intended it to be almost. Both times," I assured him. "Now, *por favor,* Azcón," I said politely, "regard carefully what I am about to do." I pulled the hat from my head, tossed it aloft, aimed the sling, and pierced the hat through when it was still some twenty paces in the air.

By this time, quite a crowd had gathered. Azcón looked about him uneasily. Always he had been accustomed to dominate the scene; the other students avoided him as a matter of good policy. Now, however, they sensed a change. Like the crowd smelling the kill in the bullring, they were exceptionally quiet, only pressing in closer so as not to miss whatever action would take place. I cannot deny that this was for me, as for the *toreador,* a moment of great triumph. While everyone watched, I aimed my sling at the bottles on the wall. The pebbles hit their targets so quickly that it seemed as if a single stone leaped from bottle to bottle, knocking all of them over. When the last bottle crashed, the students cheered.

I turned to Azcón. Immediately the shouts died down. The drama was not yet done. "I wish you now to pay close attention to what I am about to say, Azcón," I said. My voice was low, yet I knew that its message carried clearly. "If ever you or one of your group lays a hand upon me again, if ever you or one of your group speaks to me with less than unfailing courtesy, you will be buried with a stone from my sling so deep in your head no one will be able to remove it. Shall I convince you?" I raised the sling

Azcón paled. "No! No!" he said immediately, putting a hand up before his face. "I am convinced."

"Now, then," I continued. "What is my name?"

He remained silent. I reached for another stone. "Santiago Ramón y Cajal," he cried out. I turned to his followers. "My name, please?" "Santiago Ramón y Cajal," they answered obediently.

"I think," I said pleasantly, "you will remember that name always, will you not?"

They nodded. The other students encircled me,

clapping me on the shoulder, laughing, talking. How I would have welcomed this when first I came to the Institute. The bell rang, summoning us to classes. Chattering, the other boys ran off but I noticed that Azcón lingered behind. Surely he did not wish to speak with me, I thought, amazed, but this was exactly what Azcón wanted.

"You are a very stubborn fellow," he said.

"Yes. I am stubborn."

"Why?" he asked. "Why would you not give in? I would have let you alone if you had said right away . . . I mean to say, new boys must expect to be treated a little rough in the beginning. What's the harm, eh, Santiago?"

"The harm is that it makes bullies. Bullies push weaker people around. They feed upon such weakness. I have no taste for it. As you have said yourself, I am a stubborn fellow."

He put out his hand. "Will you be friends?"

I shook my head. "I am not so generous in nature that I can put behind me so quickly these past months," I replied slowly. "I do not grant friendship easily."

He shrugged his shoulders. "As you wish," he agreed and ran off to class.

That night I wrote in my letter to my brother:

> I have had a wonderful idea. I am going to write a book, which I shall illustrate, naturally. I am going to call it *Lapidary Strategy*, an important title, even impressive, is it not? This book will be

for my friends, to teach them the proper use of the sling. I am even now thinking of rules — what to do and what not to do . . .

But this project I abandoned quickly, for next morning Don Carlos detained me as I was about to leave his classroom.

"I have had a letter from your father."

I looked up and then down again. From the tone of his voice I knew that the news was bad.

"He refuses. He will not even consider the matter. And he begs that I do not encourage you. He writes that you know well his feelings about your so-called artistic talent. And if you have not made clear these feelings to me, then he must state it plainly: that I am not to interfere with his plans for his son, and so on, and so forth." Don Carlos paced the room, angrily smacking my father's letter against his hand. "I cannot imagine an educated man, a doctor, so deaf to reason. To be so rigid . . . so insensitive . . ."

What had I expected? Had I not known all along what the outcome would be? Why was I, therefore, so sick at heart? I turned and left the room, not even listening when Don Carlos cried out after me, "Santiago! Wait!" There welled up within me, as never before, such frustration, such anger, that I now became in truth what everyone at home called me — the wild one. Up to this time, I had made some effort in my classes. I was not and never had been the best of students, but from this moment on, I turned my mind away completely. I did not stay away from school altogether, but I was more often absent than present. And I led others with me, among them, and this will surprise you, Azcón and his faithful followers. I taught them to use the sling, and together we fought other bands of students. Even worse, we became involved with battling police.

They did not know for certain who we were, or that I was the ringleader, only that their lives had suddenly become disrupted. We were to them like small gnats, buzzing and stinging and generally making nuisances of ourselves. It was funny to us but hardly so to the *guardias,* who swore they would acquaint us with the interior of the jail before long.

One day, in one of our skirmishes, Azcón managed to strike one of the policemen with a pebble on the thigh. Instantly the policeman fell to the ground, swearing that he had been killed. *"Asesino!"* he groaned. Assassin, indeed! "After them! After them!" he charged his companions. Obligingly, they drew their swords and gave chase. Pausing to take aim, I let a stone fly. Even I never expected to see such results. The pebble roared through the air with such momentum that when it struck the blade of one of the pursuers, it snapped the steel, breaking it off, so that the *guardia* was left holding only the hilt of the sword which he stared at in stupefaction.

Thereafter we ran like the wind, for the police are very proud of their weapons. Now they would never give up until they found us. We scattered as soon as we were out of sight. I did not dare go back to the boarding house. Instead, I headed for the old wall just beyond the threshing floors of Cáscaro, scaled it, coming down on the other side with the help of various stones which projected from the wall, crossed the river, and hid in a grove of poplar trees.

The *guardias* captured Azcón and one other, but they did not yield the names of their companions to the police. Nonetheless, I was still afraid to go back to the boarding house and went instead to Don Carlos who listened to my tale with his lips compressed. Finally he said, "Santiago, you are a fool. Do you wish to destroy yourself completely? What do you prove by these antics?"

"I have not come here for a lecture," I said sullenly, turning to go. He caught me by the arm.

"You may stay here with me for a while," he said. "But you must promise that you will give up this childish nonsense and return to school."

When I saw how in earnest he was, I agreed. Perhaps all I needed was to feel that someone did care for me, for Santiago himself, not for some ideal that lived in another's ambition. As suddenly as I had taken up my wayward existence, I abandoned it, even going back to each of my classes. But it was no use. I had stayed away too long. I was far behind in my work; I did not even know what was being discussed. In most classes, except for Greek and religion, my presence was greeted with indifference. My Greek and religion instructors, however, regarded me with active dislike. The first despaired for my mind, the second for my soul. Both used me as a target for cutting remarks. That they were right did not help me . . . in fact, it

131

made matters worse, for how can one forgive someone who is right?

I had promised Don Carlos to attend school, but I could not curb my restlessness in these two classrooms. In the Greek class, when the instructor glared at me, I waited until he turned away and then drew *caricaturas* of him, drawings that were little better than cartoons, you understand, in which I made fun of his political beliefs. He was a strong monarchist, and often bored the students with long, tiresome speeches against the people who spoke for freedom and a constitution. Don Vicente, who taught religion, was little better. He was not a man of grace, not in appearance, not in voice, not in manner. Everything in his face was large — the nose, which was flat as well, the ears, the lips. The cheekbones were prominent, and above these cheek-bones and the large nose was one black penetrating eye and one sightless eye which Don Vicente refused to cover with a patch.

I did not draw in Don Vicente's room. Here I sat quietly — and smiled. Do you know that a smile is a weapon? Do you realize how difficult, how impossible it is to protect oneself from the smile upon the face of another? That smile was a constant torment to Don Vicente, for he was a zealot who himself never smiled, for whom the world was but a preview of the hell which all would find themselves in except, apparently, Don Vicente.

Do you think I am without faith? I am one who believes strongly in God. But the God of Don Vicente reminded me too much of my father — implacable, unbending.

Like my father, Don Vicente's God refused to listen, had no compassion. He punished. In my life so far there had been too much punishment. So I played my little game — and smiled.

Don Vicente, upon first perceiving my expression, stopped almost in the middle of a word to stare at me.

"You think I am amusing, Santiago?" he shrilled at me.

"Amusing? No, Señor, I assure you," I answered honestly.

"Ah! Then perhaps what I am saying is amusing?"

"No, Señor."

"But you smile, Santiago. Perhaps you would care to explain why, in the midst of our lesson on a serious subject, you see fit to smile."

"It was just a thought . . ."

"Better and better! While the rest of us are concerned with fire and brimstone, Santiago sits and thinks amusing thoughts. Share this amusing thought with us."

While Don Vicente spoke, his face turned pale, as if the blood were being drained from his head with anger instead of rushing to his brain. His voice, which was always shrill and nasal, grew even more piercing. Even the hair on the back of his hands seemed to bristle.

Naturally, such a situation could not last. I was expelled from the class. Having been thrown out of one class, it followed naturally that I began little by little to abandon all other classes as well, despite my promise to Don Carlos.

So the time went; the cold weather disappeared, spring arrived, bringing sunshine and warmth, and for me the prospect of summer and home. Unfortunately, it brought as well the time for final examinations.

FOURTEEN

THE DAY FINAL EXAMINATIONS began at the Institute, I made my way to school with dragging feet and reluctant heart. Should I present myself? For what purpose? What had I learned these past months? Yet to stay away was equally unthinkable. One had to attend so important an event.

I was almost near the school grounds when I noticed that the town wall which skirts the road had just been newly plastered and whitewashed. Its broad white surface tempted me. In my pocket, I began to finger the pieces of chalk and charcoal which I always kept there.

One moment, I promised myself. I will take but a moment and draw something quickly. Then I will go on to school. I tell you that I honestly meant only to make some small mark upon that wall, but some demon within me guided my hand, for almost before I myself realized what I was doing I began to make life-size *caricaturas*, cartoon drawings, if you will, of some of my instructors. A caricature is naturally not flattering to its subject, for in a caricature an artist exaggerates the worst or most conspicuous features. Such sketches are often funny but never kind. For the artist, however, they are a *diversión,* an enjoyment, a test of skill. I drew Don Carlos, and Don Antonio, and Don Jenaro. Then I devoted myself energetically to Don Vicente. Of all the caricatures, this was without doubt the most excellent. Some people seem to be born with the proper features for caricature; do you not find it so? Don Vicente's large flat nose, his cheekbones, the sightless eye — all this I rendered faithfully upon the wall. Laughing to myself, I stepped back to regard my work. At that moment, as it happened, some of the students came strolling down the road. Evidently I had been at my task longer than I realized, for the examinations, at least some, were over.

The students were in gay spirits, released from the burden of ridding themselves of the knowledge they had stuffed themselves with these past few months.

"Hey, Santiago," one called out. "You did well to stay away from school today. The examinations were *formidable.*"

"Hey! That's Don Vicente, one-eyed Vicente!" another shouted. He looked about for a stone and cast it at the wall. "That for Don Vicente!"

Immediately the others were inspired to do likewise. They threw rocks, shouting such words as I would not repeat to you.

"Stop!" I shouted.

One of the boys said with surprise, "What? Do you defend Don Vicente after the way you have acted toward him in class? Hypocrite!" he added with disgust. He picked up an especially sharp stone and hurled it with all his strength.

"No, wait. Listen," I implored, trying to catch him and some of the other students by their arms to spoil their throws.

"Go away, Santiago," they said, pushing me aside.

"My drawings," I insisted. "You are destroying my drawings."

"Go find another wall," they laughed.

While we were arguing among ourselves, a number of teachers came down the road, among them Don Vicente. One student, spying them, fell into abashed silence, a rock still in his hand. Next to him, first one, then another also stopped, some dropping their stones meekly to the ground, others making futile efforts to conceal the rocks in their hands. Don Carlos, seeing his caricature, grinned. Not so Don Vicente. His cheek twitched; his one good eye glared; a vein in his forehead throbbed. He actually wrung his hands.

"Who is responsible for this . . . this *atrocidad?*" he sputtered.

"Surely it is not an atrocity," Don Carlos said soothingly. "As a matter of fact, Vicente, it is rather well drawn. I think the artist, whoever he is — " Don Carlos was careful to keep his eyes averted from the students — "has some talent. Look at his caricature of me."

Don Vicente, however, would not be diverted. Having no sense of humor, he saw nothing amusing in the situation. Rather he was furious. His pride had been wounded, his sense of superiority attacked; he had been humiliated not only by his students but before his peers. It was not to be borne.

"I repeat," he said hoarsely, "who is the perpetrator of this vandalism? If I do not get a name in twenty seconds, I shall fail every student in my class."

With such an inducement, could anyone remain quiet? "It was Santiago," a dozen voices cried.

Don Vicente turned quickly and attempted to seize me by the scruff of my neck. I looked up and down the road. On one side, my way was blocked by the instructors, on the other by those who had just betrayed me. Before me was the wall. There was only one direction left to me, the road behind me and the field and small stream which lay beyond. Between the road and the field there ran a wide ditch whose banks on either side were covered with mud. Since it was a sunny day, I assumed these surfaces would be hard and dry. Therefore, without waiting another moment, I ran and made a mighty leap across the ditch.

"Stop him! Stop him!" Don Vicente shouted.

I wish now that someone had been able to do so, for when I landed on the other side of the ditch, the bank gave way beneath my feet. That seemingly solid surface was a sea of mud. So hard did my feet hit the bank that, before I knew what was happening, I had sunk into the mud almost up to my chest.

"Out! I command you to get out and come back," Don Vicente shrieked.

I would have liked nothing better than to get out but with every moment of struggle I sank deeper, until at last only my arms and head were visible. And almost as bad as my imprisonment in the mud was the stench that arose and gagged me.

"I cannot move," I cried.

This had become obvious by now to everyone on the other side of the bank. A few of the students, feeling sorry for me, made as if to leap across to my aid but Don Vicente once again issued an order. "I forbid you to help him," he said coldly. "Let him stay where he is and contemplate where his folly has brought him."

"But Don Vicente," one of the braver ones protested, "Santiago may drown in that mud. It is impossible for him to pull himself out."

"That is his problem, not yours. You will all leave now. There is nothing further you can do here."

The students milled about, fearful of Don Vicente, but unwilling to go off and leave me in so precarious a situation. I was truly frightened. Each time I moved, the mud made little sucking sounds. Had I lived thus far only to end my days covered with slime, a slow, tormenting death for my sins? I closed my eyes to shut out such thoughts, and thus did not see Don Carlos leap across the ditch.

"I forbid it," Don Vicente shouted after him in frustration. I believe in his anger he did not realize how dangerous my position was, for even Don Vicente, assuredly, would not wish me such harm. Don Carlos disregarded his colleague. He reached down and seized my outspread arms, covering himself with mud in the process. Bracing himself as best he could, he tugged, exerting himself to such an extent that his face grew red. Feeling himself slipping, he shouted for assistance. Instantly two of the students came across; one made it safely to the bank, the other fell somewhat short and began sliding downward into the mud. He was seized and hauled to safety before he could become mired. Now these two, along with Don Carlos, worked energetically to free me. Slowly, slowly, my body left the oozing mud until at last I stood quivering beside the others on dry land.

We four presented a sorry sight. I, of course, was smeared from head to foot. My face and even my hair were coated. I longed for nothing more than to plunge into the cleansing waters of the stream beyond and would have done so at once except that at this moment another diversion occurred. A horse and buggy were approaching, the hooves of the horse hitting the road briskly; a tall man, sitting quite erect and holding the reins easily, brought the buggy to a halt directly before the caricature of Don Vicente on the wall. His eyes swept the scene and noted everything, the drawings, the watching spectators, the instructors, my mud-stained saviors, and myself.

"Papa," I called desperately, "things are not as they seem, believe me."

"Don Justo! A word with you!" Don Vicente said hoarsely, approaching the buggy.

After one cold glance in my direction, my father descended and the two men walked off, Don Vicente gesturing wildly and my father, as usual, calm and controlled.

FIFTEEN

I HAVE DEVELOPED an instinct for somber news.
There is an atmosphere such news creates, even before
it is spoken, that one can almost reach out and touch.
Do you yourself not find that this is so? When I came
to the table for breakfast that morning, some two
weeks after I had returned in disgrace from the
Institute at Huesca, to discover my mother unusually
subdued, Pedro studying the dish before him, and my
father tight-lipped and grim, I hesitated to sit down.

My mother heaped my plate full; she firmly believes
that food overcomes all sorrows and disappointments.
When I pushed the dish aside, she said faintly, "You
must eat something, Santiago," but did not insist
further.

My father, I noticed, had already methodically
eaten. In our household, to waste food for any reason
is a grievous sin. He placed his silverware precisely in
the center of his plate, cleared his throat, and plunged
directly to the heart of the matter. "Since it is now

perfectly clear, Santiago, that you will not bend your mind to your lessons, I have decided that you will no longer go to school."

Pedro flashed me a quick glance of woe, then dropped his eyes back again to the table, like a chicken hypnotized by a seed upon the ground.

"Instead," my father continued, "you will learn a trade. I have made arrangements for you to become apprenticed to Señor Pedrín."

"The *cobbler?*" I asked with surprise.

"Since you are not a ·student, perhaps you can without too much difficulty repair shoes." The scorn in my father's voice shamed me before my mother and brother. I rose to my feet. At first I was tempted to make some flippant remark, to show that I did not care, but I was fearful that the words might sound too tearful, so I said nothing but went instead directly to my room to pack.

How shall I describe to you Señor Pedrín? One would expect a shoemaker to be small, with shoulders rounded from hunching over boots and sandals, and perhaps with narrowed, peering eyes of small vision. Señor Pedrín, let me tell you, was nothing like this at all. He was a big man of much muscle, brown-skinned, with a bullet head, a broad nose, and sharp, merry black eyes. Around his forehead he wore perpetually a handkerchief, greasy and tattered, for he perspired heavily.

Señor Pedrín was expecting me. My room was ready, he announced. As soon as I was unpacked, he had some tasks for me to do, he added. My father nodded.

"Do not spare him," my father instructed Señor Pedrín.

Señor Pedrín understood. I was not to be given special favors simply because I was the son of *el doctor*. I said nothing. What was there for me to say? That because my father did not wish me to be treated with special consideration because of his position, I suffered more than any other? For whenever my father issued this warning, teachers and others immediately reacted too strongly, being harsher with me than was absolutely necessary, to prove to themselves and to my father that no favors were being extended or could be expected.

"See that he eats whatever food is prepared," my father added, before he left. "Santiago must learn that one cannot afford to be squeamish at the table."

Señor Pedrín guffawed, a hearty snort that sounded like distant thunder rumbling over the mountain.

"We do not stand on ceremony here. Besides," he snickered, "a frightened bird is already half-trapped." He issued a series of half-choked roars of laughter that swept my father from his shop. Turning, he roared, "You there, Martín. *Pronto!* Take Santiago to his room. And do not dawdle, either of you. There is work to be done. Remember, you will find no birds in last year's nests."

Martín, another apprentice, a pale, quiet boy somewhat younger than myself, beckoned me to follow him to the back of the shop. There a stairway, narrow and crooked, stumbled upward in the dark to a landing that turned right and became a long corridor off which there were several rooms.

"What does he mean, Señor Pedrín, we will find no birds in last year's nests?" I asked curiously.

Martín opened one of the doors to reveal a tiny room with a small, high window covered by a curtain so gray and dusty it had no shape or color. In one corner there was a bed, half curtained off; opposite it was a chest of drawers. The space between the two was so narrow, I could lie on the bed and open a drawer with no difficulty. Above the chest there hung a plaster crucifix with the figure of Jesus so limp upon the cross, it made me weary just to look at it. There was not room for Martín and myself simultaneously, so Martín stayed in the open doorway.

"What did Señor Pedrín mean?" I repeated.

Martín shrugged. "Señor Pedrín has as many old sayings as a cucumber has seeds. Who knows what he means? Who listens?" That was the longest speech I ever heard Martín make.

A shout from the bottom of the stairway brought us back to the landing. Below, Señor Pedrín was waiting impatiently. "A broom in the corner does not sweep clean. *Pronto! Pronto!*"

Martín skittered down the steps and I followed. "You, there. Not so fast, young fellow," Señor Pedrín caught my arm. "A chicken is not a chicken until it is an egg." By this I soon learned he meant that, before I would be permitted to work on boots and shoes, I must first attend to the most menial tasks. To me fell the chore of emptying the slops, sweeping the shavings and bits and pieces of leather that fell to the floor, clearing the dishes from the table and washing them. That night when I went to bed, I stayed awake just long enough to stare at the crucifix above the chest and think that anyone in this household must sag with weariness. My eyes closed, and when they opened again, Martín was standing over me, already fully clothed, to inform me that Señor Pedrín expected us to rise with the sun, or before it, if we wished to be fed.

Yawning, I sat up and said I would be down directly. Still yawning, I slid sleepily into my chair at the table. Señor Pedrín, who is boisterous and charged with cheer even at so early an hour, regarded me with amusement.

"So you slept well, eh, Santiago?"

I was examining my arms closely. While I had slept the fleas had held a mass meeting upon my limbs. Señor Pedrín grinned. "*Quien duerme bien . . .*" he began.

"I know, Señor," I interrupted. "Even I know that one. 'Who sleeps well the fleas do not disturb.' "

"We shall get along, Santiago," he beamed at me. "We shall get along famously."

Once again my day was filled with the most ignoble of tasks. Between Señor Pedrín and my father, I was being punished properly. Señor Pedrín watched me closely, but I did everything that was assigned to me. I did not complain; I did not cheat on my chores. If my father expected me to wilt under this treatment, I thought stubbornly, he was mistaken.

Whenever I could, I watched both Martín and Señor Pedrín at work. Señor Pedrín was a man of much skill and a patient teacher. Time and again he corrected Martín, showing him how to hold the awl, how to trim the heels, how to sculpt the leather. One day he said to me, rather abruptly, "One does not enjoy the gravy if one cannot taste the meat." He motioned me to sit down beside him at the cobbler's bench. "I think it is time for you to begin to learn the art of shoemaking."

Do you know that shoemaking is in truth an art? For example, to make an *abotinado,* which is a high boot, requires much cunning in the hands, for the heels are quite fancy and the boot itself is decorated with a kind of filigree carved with knife and awl.

I had been forbidden the use of paint and pencils, and Señor Pedrín had obeyed my father's instructions faithfully, never permitting me to lay my hands upon paper or painting equipment, even of the most meager kind. But nothing had been mentioned about shoes and boots! Soon I began to work my own designs into the boots. As for the heels! What joy! I traced the most delicate motifs into the leather; each boot was different from the other. Lacking paper and paints, my canvas became the leather.

Señor Pedrín was delighted. The women and young girls insisted upon having their boots made only in his shop, and insisted further that young Santiago Ramón y Cajal and no other create them.

146

"I met your good father in the square this morning," Señor Pedrín said one day as I bent over my work. "I told him of your progress. He was most pleased. You do not believe that," he commented shrewdly.

"My father wished me to become a doctor," I replied. "Can he now be content that I become a cobbler?"

"It is a good trade," Señor Pedrín bristled. "True, I will never grow rich, but then he who grows wealthy in one year will live to hang by his neck in six months, eh, Santiago?"

Martín and I exchanged glances; he was as silent as ever. If he objected to my growing skill, or resented it, I did not know. Perhaps, however, in his quiet way, he enjoyed my company, for each time Señor Pedrín spouted one of his sayings, Martín and I looked at each other and grinned.

Señor Pedrín picked up a boot and examined it closely; then, seizing a pair of scissors, he snipped some threads. "You have been careless here, Santiago. Regard the unevenness of this stitching. Remember, it is a far cry between said and done. Do you know what else your good father told me? He told me to watch you at the dinner table. And why? Because I remarked about your good appetite, how you eat all that is put before you, and do you know what his reply was? 'Watch Santiago. He is not to be trusted.'"

I could feel my face flushing. I did not answer — what could I say? That I heartily disliked his cooking? That I detested certain foods? That rather than hurt his feelings I had resorted to trickery? Why did my father persist in this persecution? I was so angry my vision blurred.

"Have I your permission, Señor, to go out for a little while?" I asked. "I am not feeling too well. Perhaps some air?"

When I had first come, such a request would have been unthinkable. Now, however, Señor Pedrín was anxious to keep me content. Business, as he himself had admitted, had never been so good. I went, as always when I needed to be alone, to the river and stretched out under a willow which folded its branches gracefully to the bank, creating a silver green sanctuary that hid me from view. Tall reeds, golden and russet, marched along the banks on both sides, and between them the river sparkled its way to the horizon.

I sat and brooded, and did not know why. Curiously, in spite of my hard life at the cobbler's — and it was hard; you must not be misled — there was much that I enjoyed there. Señor Pedrín was a stern taskmaster; he could be mean in little things and cruel in big things; the food he served was a disaster; my room was but a closet. Yet he encouraged me when I worked, calling me a gifted artist, calling upon heaven to witness my skill, and whenever he was particularly pleased with one of my *abotinados* not above hugging me suddenly. The first time he pulled me close with those bearlike arms, I was astonished. The thought flashed through my mind that my father had never put his arm around me, never given me one sign of affection. But then, of course, my father hates me . . .

I did not wish to sit here any longer. My thoughts

were too heavy, too oppressive. I leaped to my feet and ran back to the shop. The willow leaves and the golden brown reeds had inspired me with a new design which I was eager to try on a pair of boots. These were for the daughter of the marquis; I wanted them to be exceptionally beautiful.

That night at supper, Señor Pedrín seemed to be observing me more than usual. For our meal, Señor Pedrín had prepared fish. It was hot in the kitchen, and the odor was overwhelming. Even Martín, who accepted everything without complaint, turned his head away when Señor Pedrín brought the dish to the table. The eye of the fish stared at me unblinkingly.

"*Por favor*, Señor," I said faintly. "I am not very hungry tonight."

"Not hungry? Of course you are hungry." He began to carve the fish, then, with knife and fork poised in the air, he laughed. "I will tell you a story," he shouted merrily. "It is a story of a fool and two wise men. The fool was sitting down to eat a fish he had caught when the two wise men came along. Being a gentleman, the fool invited the others to share his simple meal. 'You are most gracious, Señor,' the first wise man said. 'I ask only one thing, that you do not give me the head.' 'It is an honor to dine with you, Señor,' said the second wise man. 'I care not what I eat, so long as it is not the tail.' The two wise men looked at each other and smiled, expecting that the fool would give them the part in between. 'Señores,' the fool swore, 'never would I give you that which you cannot eat.' So he cut the fish into three pieces. Before

149

the wise men could help themselves, the fool put the head of the fish on a dish and gave it to the man who did not want the tail. He gave the tail to the man who did not want the head. And while the two wise men sat and stared at him, the fool ate what was in between."

Señor Pedrín's roar of laughter shook the table. "Who wishes the head and who wishes the tail?"

I started to rise. Martín pushed his chair back, meaning to leave the table also. But have I not told you that Señor Pedrín has a meanness in him?

"You will dine with me, or I shall break your necks." We subsided in our chairs, and waited helplessly for our portions. With the fish, Señor Pedrín was serving turnips. I do not know how you feel, but to me a turnip is a most unfortunate vegetable.

"Señor," I pleaded.

"Eat!"

Martín closed his eyes and swallowed quickly, but I am not Martín. I am Santiago Ramón y Cajal, a mule when I am pushed. I pretended to take a mouthful. Then, when Señor Pedrín rose to get himself another bottle of wine, I took the fish and the turnips and slid them into the pocket of my trousers.

When I had first tasted Señor Pedrín's cooking and realized what the future held for me, I had sewn a special lining into this pocket. Many of Señor Pedrín's less edible dishes had landed there, and never had I been caught. When the fish and the turnips were safely hidden, I pretended to be scraping my dish, using a piece of bread to mop it clean. Martín had not

150

seen me; his eyes were still shut. Señor Pedrín had his back to me. I stood up, pushing my chair back.

"And where are you going, young Santiago?" he boomed at me.

"See, I have finished. I will go out for a moment for some air, and then I will go to bed," I said innocently. His large hand flew out and grasped my ear.

"You will go out when pigs fly," he bellowed. "Empty your pocket. Empty it!" Martín's eyes flew open, and grew wide as I put the fish and turnips, now the most unappetizing mess you can imagine, back on the dish. "Now," Señor Pedrín inquired, "will you eat with or without my assistance, Santiago?"

I lowered my head and dug my fork into the cold, congealed food. I had just lifted it to my lips when there was a loud knocking on the door.

"Pedrín! Pedrín! Are you there? Open up! I have news!" a voice shouted.

Pedrín raced from the kitchen, Martín and I right behind him, through the shop to the front door. Pedrín flung it open.

"Pedrín! The revolution has begun," a man said excitedly. "The generals are rebelling against Queen Isabella. The monarchy is falling."

"We have had great news," another called out. "The army of liberators is marching toward Linás de Marcuello."

Señor Pedrín forgot about the fish and turnips. He and the others made their way to the plaza, where others from our village were already gathered. Martín and I followed. Such excitement did not often come to

Ayerbe. We had heard that the people were revolting against the Queen, and many of the villagers strongly supported the common cause. But always before the government was something remote. Now at last the outside world was reaching us here in our remote Aragonese village.

Watching the people, and listening to them argue, I suddenly wondered to myself, what would the peasants gain — the head, the tail, or everything in between? I did not know, and I was frightened.

SIXTEEN

Each morning I worked for Señor Pedrín, I had to be awakened by Martín and forced from my bed. Not so this morning. I had lain sleepless most of the night, caught up in the excitement of the times. Never had I been much interested in politics — Madrid was remote, Queen Isabella a name, and the insurrection of her generals gossip much garbled by the time it reached us in Ayerbe. I knew of course that for the most part our villagers supported the rebels; my father, as I have mentioned — have I not? — was a stern moralist. He despised the queen for her flagrant love affairs, her willfulness in granting much power to stupid, inefficient men simply because they were her lovers. The villagers were angered because her forces shot down those who desired a constitution and participation in government. There were loyalists in our village, however, as there must have been in many other towns: Mayor Pavía, for one, and some of the *guardia*, of course.

The night before I had listened carefully, trying to sort truth from the rumors. The only tidbit I could finally seize upon as fact regarded the liberal army. They had been billeted at Murillo and Riglos, on either side of the Gállego River, overnight. Now they were marching, even as I lay in my bed, toward Linás de Marcuello, a small village just north of Ayerbe.

I dressed quickly and ran downstairs. Martín and Señor Pedrín had already had breakfast.

"Eat quickly," Señor Pedrín said. "Then we will go to the Plaza Baja. General Manso de Zúñiga is passing through Ayerbe this morning."

"I beg of you, Señor," I stammered, "I am truly not hungry. May I go to the plaza?"

"I can see that no work will be done this day," he said, grudgingly. "Well, no matter." He sighed philosophically. "He who loses a day gains a memory. Be off with you then. You, too, Martín."

We bolted from the room before Señor Pedrín could change his mind, but we needn't have worried; he was as anxious as we to hasten to the plaza. Juan and Francisco were there, as well as Lope and the others, all of whom greeted me with enthusiasm. It was only a matter of moments before the loyalist troops appeared, a full column of infantry preceded by at least fifty mounted soldiers led by General de Zúñiga. To watch men on horses marching in formation arouses the blood. Not a boy in that crowd, including myself, failed to envy the cavalry, proud and haughty above the people, their armor and plumed helmets glittering in the sun. The hooves of the horses stirred the dust which spiraled upward; the tiny particles danced in shafts of sunlight and seemed to surround each cuirassier with a luminous halo, like the nimbus around the moon on certain clear nights.

Behind the cavalry, the foot soldiers marched in perfect formation, their faces carefully wooden. A command was issued; the men halted. In all that army, not a word was spoken, even while they rested. They knew full well how this impressed the villagers.

Mayor Pavía approached the general.

"How may we serve you?" he asked. The mayor was excited, but he pretended great calm. Now those villagers who supported the insurrectionists would see the might of the queen and the importance of the mayor.

"My men need rations," the general rasped. "See to it at once."

"It shall be done." There is a saying among our people: Why rush? Tomorrow is still a long way off. Ordinarily, even the mayor would not hurry. But this was not a day like other days. The loyalists among the people brought food as fast as they could, but even this did not satisfy General de Zúñiga, for he gave his men but little time to eat, so anxious was he to meet with the liberal forces at Linás de Marcuello. Before long, the command was given. As splendidly as they arrived, the queen's forces left the plaza.

The villagers, left behind in the square, were not desirous of returning to their various tasks. Instead, they gathered in small groups to relive the excitement of the morning. Small, fierce arguments raged between those who supported the queen and those who wished to see the monarchy topple. There were angry comments and hints of reprisal against those who had been active in the rebellion. Who, seeing the strength and arrogance of the queen's troops, could doubt that the battle at Linás would soon be over? Some of the younger men who had joined the rebel forces were even now hiding in the hills, fearful of what would happen to them once General de Zúñiga's army conquered the insurgents.

Suddenly a hush fell over the square. The sound of battle reverberated from Linás, a muted, distant cadence, like thunder rumbling far off in the mountains.

"The fighting has begun!" someone said.

Lope and my other friends gathered round me.

"I wish we could see the fighting," Francisco said, digging his shoe into the dust.

"Me, too," Juan agreed.

"Why do we stand here and wish?" I asked impatiently. "Linás is not so far as all that."

"But the battle has already begun," Claudio objected.

"It has begun, but it will be a long time before it is over," I insisted. With that, I raced from the plaza, with my friends following at my heels. Never have fields been crossed so quickly! We ran until the beating of our hearts thudded in our ears and our breath was sucked in in long, shuddering gasps, but to me it felt as if we moved in a sea of molasses. Always ahead, however, to spur us on was the dull, insistent sound of firing.

We reached Linás almost exhausted. There we

156

scaled a small hill, just south of the village, from the top of which we could peer down and watch the battle below. How can I describe to you the scene that presented itself to our eyes? Often I had drawn clashing soldiers amid heroic battles, on paper, on walls, on the sides of barns; men fired with the zeal of war, proud, majestic, lordly. Now at last I saw the reality, and my heart sickened against war for all time.

The queen's troops were in retreat, moving back toward Ayerbe. Skirting the foot of the mountain range, the rebels drove the loyalists before them, no longer firing upon them, merely herding them as our shepherds guide the goats and sheep.

"I cannot see," Lope complained. The road, winding beneath us, was half-hidden. We left our hill to climb another, one which afforded us a clear view of the road.

"Madred de Dios!" Juan whispered as the men filed silently by beneath us. The cavalry, only this morning wreathed in sunshine, their swords sending blinding flashes of light, were now on foot. Some had lost their horses; others had given their mounts to carry the wounded. Jolted on the rough surface, these moaned and bled while the cuirassiers held them in place, their own faces reflecting pain and confusion. The immaculate uniforms were covered with dirt and blood; here and there helmets were either dented or missing.

"Look there!" Lope pointed. "The general! I think he is dying!"

Only once before had I beheld a dead man, Father Félipe in the bell tower the day lightning struck the

schoolhouse. Now, even to my inexpert eyes, it was obvious that General de Zúñiga's life was slipping fast. He still sat upon his horse, but if it had not been for his faithful aide who held him securely erect, the general would have fallen. The aide propped de Zúñiga up with fierce pride, though he himself was bleeding, ignoring the cries of the wounded and the disorderly, shuffling, stumbling steps of the troops around him.

"Hey, Santiago, *qué pasa?*" Francisco said with surprise as I rose to leave.

"I am going back to Ayerbe," I said. "I have seen enough."

"But . . ."

"I have seen enough!" I shouted. I descended the hill, away from the road, and fled back across the clean sweep of the fields. I wanted nothing more at this moment than to escape to the river, to the tranquillity of the quiet waters and the tree-shrouded banks. Yet strangely, when at last I came to Ayerbe, I directed my footsteps home. But how transformed! My father, anticipating the need, had converted the barn into a small hospital, corraling beds from the villagers — beds and blankets and sheets and pillows. A number of women, under my mother's direction, were busily tearing sheets into strips for bandages. I came closer, feeling suddenly awkward and in the way. Just then my father looked up.

"Ah, Santiago," he said quietly, as if he had been waiting for me. "You are just in time. I need you."

SEVENTEEN

I DO NOT KNOW what I thought the practice of medicine was, or my father's role in it. Perhaps it meant to me no more than binding up a farmer's arm after some mischance with a tool, or splinting the leg of an active boy fallen from a tree, or attendance upon those mysterious ailments to which the women seemed heir to, both in Ayerbe and in the surrounding towns. Never had I seen my father as doctor, nor, I admit, had I cared to do so. Now, however, here in our improvised hospital, the father disappeared and in his place there was only Don Justo, *el médico*. He issued orders to the women — how to bathe, how to dress wounds — remarking sharply when they were sloppy or failed to wash their hands before and after tending patients; he kept Pedro and myself at his side, to hand him instruments, to press packed strips of sheets against bleeding vessels, to watch how he treated the wounded. And always he talked, a low, steady stream of information. At first Pedro and I felt faint and in urgent need to run behind the barn to throw up, but my father forbade it, his voice stinging and severe, reminding us that in the time it took for us to indulge our weakness, a man could die. I tried to shut out his lectures, then found that, in spite of myself, I was becoming interested.

The priests walked among the beds, giving last rites where needed, praying with others gravely ill. The soldiers were the wounded of both sides, loyalist and rebel, but my father made no distinction between them, nor, for the most part, did the priests. Father Miguel, however, who was a staunch loyalist, approached my father as he made his rounds.

"Don Justo, if you please. A moment of your time."

My father paused, waiting.

"Since there are so many wounded, and you can but tend to so few," Father Miguel murmured, "surely those who serve our gracious queen should take precedence over the others." He would have continued, but my father interrupted him brusquely.

"You are the priest and I am the doctor. Let us not confuse our roles, Father Miguel."

"I am merely . . ."

"Father, you are wasting my time, which I cannot afford. Do not interfere, or I shall be forced to forbid you entrance here."

"Forbid *me?* A priest of God's house?" Father Miguel said, shocked.

"Then go to God's house and pray. Here there are no sinners or saints, only the wounded and the dying. Santiago, see to Sebastián Medina." My father walked away, leaving Father Miguel with his mouth still open, while I hurried to Sebastián's side.

161

Sebastián Medina was from Riglos, one of the men who had early joined the rebels. I had seen him several times when he came to the fiestas in the plaza at Ayerbe. What a *charro*, a dandy, he was then! Every girl looked at him, pretending not to be looking, for Sebastián in ordinary clothes was handsome enough, but at fiesta time, a dazzling sight. His eyes were feverishly bright when I neared his bed. His hands, hot and dry, seized mine. "Hey, Santiago," he whispered. "Do you know what I wish you to tell my mother? When I die, I want to be buried in my fiesta clothing, the velvet waistcoat — write this down, Santiago . . ."

"You are not going to die, Sebastián," I muttered.

". . . and the waistband, not the silk one, the one with the square silver buttons, she knows which one, and also the shoes with the silver buckles. And the golden buckle for my collar. Are you writing this down? Doctor," he rambled, clutching my hands. "The saints will preserve you. These are the hands of mercy." He raised my fingers to his lips. "The Blessed Virgin keep these healing hands from harm."

"Sebastián," I protested. "I am not a doctor. It is me, Santiago."

"Do not exchange words with him," my father's voice said from behind me. "He does not know what you are saying or what he is saying. You would do better to bathe him with cool water to bring the fever down. Doctor!" my father added before he moved on.

At the next bed, a young man was propped up, a

162

bandage around his head, watching me as I tended to Sebastián.

"He is quite a man, *el doctor*," he commented. "You must be proud to have such a one for a father." I did not reply. "Certainly he is proud of you."

I turned and stared at him.

"What? Are you surprised? Then you do not have eyes in your head," he went on easily. "I have been watching. He teaches you, each time he stops for one of us. All the time, he explains what he is doing and why he is doing it. And he sees that you understand and absorb. You will be a good doctor, it is apparent; but then, why not? As the twig is bent, so grows the tree, eh?"

"You seem to be recovering quickly," I said rudely.

He shook his head. "For which I thank God. I am finished with war, I tell you. From this day on, let them say of me, 'This one ran away.' Much better than to have them shed a few tears and say, 'On this spot he died.' Did you see us when we marched into the Plaza Baja? I was one of the cuirassiers. Important, no? Sitting up there on my gallant horse, I looked around and I thought, we will go and stamp out those few rebels and then we will come back heroes, and the girls will flock around us. A pretty picture. Do you know what really happened, there in Linás?"

I dipped the cloth in the cool water. How quickly it became warm when I applied it to Sebastián's burning forehead.

"We advanced, in squadron formation, all glitter and polish, a sight *formidable*. But the rebels were not impressed. They were waiting for us in the hills, carefully hidden. And our good general — is he dead? Well," he shrugged his shoulders when I nodded, "even generals must die sometimes, I suppose. Hearing the shots from the hills, what does our general do, eh? He orders us to advance into the valley. To advance! And when we hesitated, like sensible men, what does he do? He whips his horse forward, shouting, *'Adelanto, hombres!'* And we, like madmen, follow him. A handful of rebels and they cut us to pieces. Still, we managed to cut down a few ourselves. Like this poor devil. And what does it all amount to in the end? The queen sits on her throne and plays her games. Or, God willing, she will seek refuge with the Empress Eugénie of France. And men will have died for nothing. Ah well, I suppose each of us is as God has made us, and will be disposed of as God sees fit."

I touched my hand to Sebastián's forehead. Did I imagine it, or had the fever abated somewhat? Yes. He felt a little cooler. I summoned my mother.

"Mama!" I whispered. "Continue to bathe him with cool water each half hour. But keep him well covered. He must not be allowed to become chilled."

"See?" the other young man said chattily. "It is as I have observed. You will be a good doctor."

My father beckoned to me at that moment.

"I need you to assist me at surgery," he said. "Call Pedro."

"He is so tired. Can he not rest a little while longer?" I asked.

My father regarded me keenly. "And you, Santiago? You are not weary?"

Until my father mentioned it, I had not realized I was so fatigued that I feared to sit down, even for a moment, lest I fall asleep. "You will have an opportunity to lie down as soon as we finish with this next patient," he said. "Unless you feel you are not sufficiently alert to be of assistance?"

"I am alert enough, Papa."

Then my father did something I shall remember the rest of my days. He touched me briefly on the shoulder, gently, and smiled, a whisper of warmth in his eyes that came and went so quickly I was unsure I had seen it. I stumbled after him, afraid, now that the suggestion had been made, that I would not be able to keep my eyes open. But watching my father's skilled hands, and listening to his patient explanation of all that he was doing, I was roused to wakefulness again. When he was finished, however, he insisted that I go to the house to rest.

"You cannot serve a patient well if you are in danger of becoming a patient yourself," he insisted.

"And what of you, Papa?" I questioned. "You have carried the whole burden yourself. Should you not also lie down for a few hours?"

"Do you concern yourself for me?" he asked, and the wonder in his voice brought a flush to my cheeks.

"I will not stay away long," I replied abruptly and went hastily from the barn, certain that once I was stretched out on my own bed again, I would sink into a timeless, dreamless sleep. But sleep did not come. I lay awake long, staring at the ceiling, remembering my father's surprise. And when sleep finally caught me unaware, it was fitful and greatly disturbed. I do not know how long I slumbered, only that I sat up abruptly, my heart pulsing, as if I had run a race. "What is it?" I cried out, hearing someone moving about.

"Sh-h-h! Santiago. Do not be alarmed," my brother Pedro said. "Father wishes you to come at once. Something has happened."

"Something has happened?" I repeated, still stupefied with sleep. "What do you mean, something has happened?"

"There has been a skirmish close to Plasencia, and some men have been killed. Father wishes us to go with him to collect the bodies."

Plasencia is a village some little way south of Ayerbe, on the road one takes to Huesca, as you are perhaps aware.

"Are you sure that Papa wishes us to go with him?" I asked, as we went down the steps.

"Would you like to question him?" Pedro answered.

"Do you think I am afraid? Certainly I will ask him." And to show Pedro that I was one who kept his word, when we climbed into the wagon, I said to my father, "What has happened, Papa? Who are these men who have died at Plasencia?"

My father snapped the reins and made a small clicking sound with his tongue. I thought at first he would not reply, but after a long moment he said,

"There was a battle between a group of smugglers and some carbineers." Carbineers are the soldiers who carry the small rifles; they are often attached to the infantry, frequently serving as an escort, particularly if there is some movement of cargo or other valuables. "I understand from one of the soldiers that they came upon the smugglers carrying contraband just as they were attempting to cross the Pyrenees. The carbineers and infantry seized the contraband. In the skirmish, one of the smugglers was killed."

"And so, naturally," Pedro interrupted with excitement, "the smugglers swore revenge."

"Naturally," my father agreed with amusement. "The smugglers followed the infantry, staying well behind so that the carbineers could not see them. Then, when they passed Ayerbe, the infantry for some reason or other galloped on, leaving the carbineers some distance behind with the wagons of contraband. True, the carbineers are fast men with the rifle, but even a dozen carbineers are no match for a group of smugglers determined to recover booty and wreak vengeance."

Beside me on the wagon seat, Pedro wriggled and sighed, as absorbed as if he were listening to me in the hideaway on Señor Cuideras's roof reading from *The Count of Monte Cristo!* "Go on, Papa," he urged. "Then what happened?"

"When the smugglers saw that the infantry had vanished some distance ahead, they fell upon the carbineers, who by this time had grown careless. They killed seven of the riflemen and drove off the others. Then they loaded the contraband on their horses and disappeared."

"Was it one of the riflemen who came to fetch you, Papa?" I wondered.

"What was the contraband they were smuggling? Was it gold, Papa, or diamonds? Perhaps it was diamonds," Pedro announced. "Diamonds are more precious than gold, are they not?"

"Since I have neither one nor the other, I cannot say," my father said indifferently. "Yes, it was one of the riflemen."

We said no more, each of us occupied with his own musings, with perhaps only my father fully aware of what we would find when we reached Plasencia.

When you are young, you do not think of death, or worry about the fragility of life. The days spin themselves out into weeks and months and years, and always time stretches ahead. Yet life can be quenched as quickly as a dry leaf is crumpled in the hand or ground underfoot, may flicker as unsteadily as a candle's flame.

I do not know if what I saw of death that night impressed me profoundly, but suddenly I had great respect for the task my father had set for himself — to fight with every fiber of his being for the life of his patients. The seven men lay as they fell. I had expected their faces to be violent, for they had died violently, but all seemed curiously at peace.

"Their faces are not distorted, Papa," I said, some-

168

what hesitantly, for I did not wish him to think I searched their expressions macabrely.

"Did you expect to find their death pangs written in their features? That is for story books," my father replied, glancing down somberly. "In death, the muscles relax. What has gone before is of little matter finally. Let us place them in the wagon now."

"Where are the other carbineers, the ones that got away?" Pedro asked, peering about. "Why have they not come to help their fallen comrades?"

"They have gone to give chase to the smugglers, I suppose. Or to report to their commanding officers. It is idle to stand here and wonder. We have work to do, Pedro. Let us be about it as quickly as possible. There is still much to be done."

Silently, the three of us set about our grim task. The way back to Ayerbe was not spent in story telling, of that you may be sure. My father was bent upon returning to Ayerbe as quickly as possible; Pedro and I sat, heads hunched into our shoulders, uncomfortably aware of the silent cargo we carried home.

When we reached Ayerbe and home, my father sent Pedro into the house and instructed him to go to bed. I started to go with Pedro, but my father held out a restraining hand. "Not you, Santiago. I must perform autopsies tonight, and I wish you to help me."

Pedro melted into the darkness, happy to be released.

"I know nothing of such things," I said with horror. "How can I help you?"

"You will see," my father replied. "Come, now," he added sharply, seeing my face. "You have seen much these past few days. And you have learned much, more than you will ever learn from books. Tonight, you will learn even more, and what you learn will stay with you. These are lessons you will never forget."

He wheeled away, never doubting for a moment that I would come after him. Sickened, I stayed where I was, but then, as my father knew I would, I followed him slowly.

EIGHTEEN

WHEN I AWOKE next morning, I became slowly aware of the sound of voices below, one of which, I realized, belonged to Señor Pedrín. Señor Pedrín! I sat up, stunned. I had forgotten completely my duties; since I had left to witness the triumphant parade of the queen's soldiers in the Plaza Baja, I had not returned to the cobbler's shop. That Martín had dutifully once again resumed his place at the bench I did not for a moment doubt. But I had been so swept up in helping my father, we both had not at any time, for obvious reasons, remembered that I was still apprenticed to Señor Pedrín.

Dressing quickly, I ran part way down the steps in time to overhear what Señor Pedrín was saying.

"That boy of yours is a gem," Señor Pedrín informed my father earnestly. My eyes flew open, wide! Never had anyone so described me before. A gem? Me? He could not mean Santiago Ramón y Cajal! "I have had many boys like Martín, good, honest boys, but never one like your son. He is an artist in leather. Since he has been with me these few weeks, my trade has increased. Important people come to my shop, and they ask for Santiago's work. You are sure, Don Justo, that you will not reconsider? There is a great future for Santiago in boots."

"The great future I wish for my son is in medicine," my father replied, "but whether this will happen remains yet to be seen."

"Patience, Don Justo. Patience," Señor Pedrín roared, "and the mulberry leaf will someday turn into silk." He turned to go, then was struck by another thought. "Surely Santiago could study in my house. I would find him a little table for his books, and at the end of the workday, I would see to it that he went upstairs to his room and opened them."

"You are most gracious, Señor, but the study I have in mind for Santiago is best accomplished here."

I had by now descended the steps and entered the room. My father, seeing me, said, "Señor Pedrín has been waiting for you. When you are finished with your day's tasks, you are to come home promptly. We have much to do."

"Yes, Papa."

I wondered what my father was planning, hoping that I would not again be called upon to help in further autopsies. This funereal task had sent me reeling into the night air several times, and once I had declared passionately that I would not and could not return to the dissecting table. However, as you perhaps suspect, my father's will had dominated.

When I returned to Señor Pedrín's shop, Martín greeted me with the news that the Countess of Parcent had been most irritated with me. She had come twice in my absence for the new boots I had promised would be ready for a special hunting party that would soon take place on the vast grounds of the Parcent castle in Gurrea de Gállego. The countess was but fourteen years of age, but always she spoke to me as if I were a dolt, talented perhaps in the craft of bootmaking, but somewhat stupid, or else why would the son of the doctor be an apprentice in this shop? She addressed herself to me in simple language, slowly, with her voice raised a bit, for I might be deaf as well as retarded.

I was greatly amused, and played my part rather well, I thought, bending my body humbly, tilting my head to one side, and making little odd sounds. Once she looked in my eyes and frowned thoughtfully. I half-expected her to say that she saw through my game, but instead she repeated her instructions that she wished the heels of her new boots to be more daintily curved than the last time. When she went out the door, I burst into laughter.

"There is much work to do," Senor Pedrin said. "And since you must report home to your good father this evening, please to begin at once."

Even as my fingers worked out the intricate design, some unusual fretwork on the toe cap, my mind was busy speculating. What studies did my father have in mind for me? More Latin? Some medical task? All day I was in a fever of impatience to know how my father proposed to use up the little free time the summer still held.

After supper, my father and I retired to his study.

He sat behind a long table, upon which were piled books and papers in orderly fashion: my father, as you know, is a most methodical man. I took a chair opposite him. For a long moment neither of us spoke. If we had stayed all evening in that room, I would not have begun the conversation, for I had no idea in which direction to go. At last my father began.

"I have decided to send you back to school, this time to Zaragoza. Do not interrupt," he held up his hand. "Before you go back, however, I think it is time you stopped, if I may sound like Señor Pedrín, hammering nails with your head." Among our people, this was a fancy way of pointing out one's obstinate nature. "I have observed how you worked with me among the wounded and dead. You will be a doctor." Again my father raised his hand, as if I had protested, although I had in truth not even moved upon my chair. "You have the intelligence, the hands, and the quality to be a surgeon. That you are ignorant is your own fault. But while you are still at home, I will undertake to teach you much that you cannot learn from books. I have also seen how quickly you can learn, Santiago, in other ways, and I have come to the conclusion that you are a 'visual.' "

"I do not understand, Papa," I said, puzzled.

"There are those who cannot learn in the usual way, through lectures or a teacher's classroom work. You are such a one. However, when I spoke to you when we worked together among the wounded, when I described each step that I did, I noted how quickly you understood what was demonstrated. Therefore I propose that we will work together visually. We will begin with anatomy."

"Anatomy? What do I know of anatomy?" I objected.

"At the moment, nothing. By the end of the summer, you will know a great deal. You may find the study of bones somewhat boring at first, but without anatomy, you can have no knowledge of medicine. Too many of our doctors, unfortunately, have applied themselves so poorly to this subject they are not fit even to tend to animals. Since you are to be a surgeon, it is not too soon for your lessons to begin."

I stared at my father with blank eyes. A surgeon? Me? Who had difficulty breathing at the sight of some grievous wound? Surely not! Why was my father so possessed of this notion? He spoke of my stubbornness; was he not the one who was driving nails with his head?

"You wish me to study some book tonight?" I asked dully.

"You do not pay strict attention, Santiago," he replied with severity. "Have I not just told you that you are not one to learn from books? You will need books, certainly, but along with that, you must have direct anatomical information."

"How are we to do that?"

"When all are asleep in the house, you and I are going to the cemetery."

I clutched the arms of my chair.

"The cemetery?" I repeated after him in a whisper. "Surely not the cemetery!"

"We need bones," my father said practically. He stood up. The matter having been settled, as far as my father was concerned, there was nothing further to discuss. "I suggest that you go to your room and rest; sleep if you can. I will wake you when it is time to leave."

How supremely calm he was. Rest? Sleep? With such a project looming before us? I went slowly up the steps, wondering desperately how I could get out of going, knowing all the while that there was no escape. Pedro was sitting cross-legged on his bed, waiting eagerly.

"What did Papa say? What has gone wrong now? Are you finished with shoemaking?" My poor brother, so full of questions to which I could not respond, for my father had cautioned me against revealing our proposed activity to anyone, even to Pedro. I thought of my father's determination for me to study anatomy and of the night's adventure that still lay ahead. "Go to sleep, Pedro," I replied crossly. "I am too tired to talk." I turned my back to him, pretending to yawn deeply.

"Are you angry with me, Santiago?"

"Por amor de Dios!" I snapped. "I am not angry. Go to sleep!"

I lay glaring at the blank wall, ashamed that I was so impatient with Pedro. Was it his fault that matters had taken so unexpected a turn? Had I so many friends that I could thrust aside the one true, steadfast person who gave from his heart without question or the need for thanks? I turned back. "Listen, Pedro, I am sorry," I began, then stopped. He was fast asleep.

He was still sleeping when my father came to the door.

"Santiago," he whispered. "Are you awake?"

I jumped from the bed immediately. Pedro stirred, muttered something and turned over, but slept on. I had not undressed; therefore I was prepared to leave the house at once. We stole down the steps and out of the house. Looking up, I saw how the moon rode serenely in the blue black sky; the stars glittered cold and remote; a small breeze filled the night with its whispers. My father paid no heed to such things; he forged on ahead quickly. I caught up with him and said urgently, "Papa, what if we are seen?"

"Who is abroad at this hour of the night?" he replied. "And who would question the doctor?"

The cemetery was a little way out beyond the limits of the village. My father was right; no one was about. Certainly the cemetery was deserted, save for those who lay eternally silenced, indifferent to the living world.

I must explain to you that our cemetery is enclosed within walls, and that to enter one goes through an iron gate wide enough for the passage of a carriage. Every night Señor Rodrigo Passera, who is both the gravedigger and the custodian, carefully locks the gate behind him when he leaves. He is a round man — his body is round, his head is round, his face is round. His eyes, which are merry and inquisitive, peer out over round, flushed cheeks. His nose, which is as red as his face, is somewhat bulbous; his lips are thick and in constant movement. Señor Passera never ceases talking. He addresses the living and the dead with equal pleasure. Oftentimes, when my friends and I have passed the cemetery, we have heard Señor Passera's voice in jovial one-sided conversations.

"The gate is locked," I said happily, having tried to push it open. "We will have to go back, Papa. Or shall I wake Señor Passera?"

I was not so clever as I thought. My father merely said sardonically, "What, Santiago? Have you never climbed a wall?"

"But what about you, Papa?" For me to scale a wall is one thing, but surely such an activity is not fitting to the dignity of one such as my father. But he had already leaped and caught an overhanging branch and was swinging agilely in the air. In a matter of moments, he was atop the wall, beckoning me to follow. While I was climbing, he jumped down on the other side of the wall. Without waiting, he hurried on through the cemetery. Never have I moved so quickly, for I had no wish to be left behind. I have my share of bravery, but I admit to you I also have my fears. The headstones loomed up at me; the statues watched with blank, sculptured eyes. The moonlight created paths of light around which the darkness appeared blacker and more menacing.

"Papa," I whispered. "I do not think we will need the bones. I am sure I can study anatomy in books."

My father did not answer, but stopped so suddenly I almost collided with him. "Good! We shall find what we need here."

I looked down, drew a deep breath, turned my head away and, fascinated, repelled, with an uneasy twisting sensation boring upward from my stomach to my throat, looked again. We were standing at a small pit, little more than a hollow in the ground, in which a jumble of assorted bones lay scattered, here a skull, there a hand, an arm, a leg. It was, my father explained briskly, the result of overcrowdedness. Some of the very old graves had been dug up, the ancient bones cast aside, to make room for the new dead.

My father kneeled to his gruesome task, selecting his samples with professional detachment — a well-formed cranium, a thigh bone, a pelvic bone. One by one he placed his finds in a sack which he had brought from home. I, too, filled a sack. My hands were trembling; however, my father did not comment.

I felt a great sadness. Once these had been living beings. Now their forgotten skeletons lay half-exposed in the gravelly soil, weeds thrusting upward through the gaping holes, vines wrapping themselves in and around the human debris, thistles ringing a skull with a ghostly crown.

"We have enough," my father said finally. Placing our sacks over our shoulders, we retraced our steps. I knew it was only imagination, but it seemed to me, as the bones rubbed against one another as I walked, that I could hear sighs and distant voices keening. Nor did this sensation subside even after we had once again climbed the wall and went quickly home through the silent night.

NINETEEN

How strange a turning one's life can take. Even if a gypsy had foretold my future, I would not have believed her.

Next morning I went off to my duties at Señor Pedrín's shop. Not by a single word or sign did my father refer to our nighttime marauding when I came to the breakfast table. He reminded me only that studies would begin as soon as I returned home — no more.

Much to my surprise, when I entered the shop, there was no sign of Martín. In his place there sat a young giant of a man, a regular lout of a fellow, with a shock of fair hair that sprang upward and an eye that had a tendency to drift companionably toward the other eye, a condition that made it impossible for me to look at him squarely. He was much older than either Martín or myself. As soon as he saw me, he jumped to his feet, leaned across the bench, and pumped my hand up and down vigorously. His voice, which boomed forth as loudly as Señor Pedrín's, was rough and rasping, but I soon discovered that he was a most obliging, good-natured, although somewhat simple person.

"This is Mariano Panza," Señor Pedrín beamed. "He is the new apprentice. Martín has been summoned home; his mother is gravely ill. Mariano has good hands. We will soon teach him all we know, eh, Santiago?"

"It will be an honor to learn from the son of the great *médico*," Mariano said courteously.

I took my place beside him, examining a piece of leather with a critical eye. For a while, Mariano said nothing, then he poked me in the ribs and said knowingly, "I have heard much of the wild one."

"What have you heard?" I asked, apprehensive lest some new tidbit would soon be carried to my father.

"One hears what one hears," he laughed, and said no more.

Mariano was eager to learn. He was not one to learn easily or quietly, and I was not too patient a teacher. But it was not possible to grow angry with him.

"I am a dolt," he cried. "You are a saint, Santiago. Only a saint would show me again and again what to do." In my role as saint, what else could I do?

When I returned home, however, I was no longer teacher but student. While I was gone, my father had set up a dissecting table in the pigeon house, along with several books on anatomy, and a variety of surgical tools.

182

"We will begin. Examine this skull. How many cavities does the skull contain?" He tapped the skull with a small pointed stick. "Two cavities enclose the eyes . . ."

"There is also a nasal cavity," I said cautiously.

"Note, please, Santiago, that there are two chambers in the nasal cavity, which is divided by the septum."

"The oral cavity," I continued to recite.

"Which contains the bones of the jaw and maxillae, palatine, and sphenoid bones."

At first I felt rebellious; what was I doing in this place examining bits and pieces of the skeletal structure which holds man together? However, as time progressed, my interest was caught. I marveled at the intricacy and wonder of the human body. In addition, my father's enthusiasm was such that it would have been most difficult not to respond. No detail, however minute, escaped him and, consequently, me.

I think my father would have gone on all night, but my eyes grew heavy, my lids drooped, and once I swayed, half-asleep.

"We will continue tomorrow," my father said reluctantly.

So began two Santiagos — during the day, shoemaker's apprentice; at night, student of anatomy.

By day, Mariano claimed my attention. He was in love, or rather, he was a man in love with being in love. No sooner did he see a pretty girl than he swore to me that he was dying of passion.

"I will send her a note," he cried. "What girl can resist a love letter?"

"Mariano, *por favor,* write your letter and be done talking about it," I begged.

"No, I have changed my mind. Why should I send her a letter? She will laugh."

"Why will she laugh?" I asked, surprised.

"Do I know why women do the things they do?" he snapped.

"Man lives either to shiver or perspire," Señor Pedrín now bellowed at us. "If you don't mind, begin the perspiration!"

Thus silenced, we fell to our work. There was no further conversation, for Señor Pedrín watched us with vigilance, but from time to time I could feel Mariano staring at me fixedly, and if I chanced to look up, his face took on the expression of a dog eager to please his master.

"There," I said finally. "The boots are finished."

"Let me see them." Señor Pedrín took them, holding them aloft, turning them this way and that. "Ah-h-h! *Qué bello!* These are worthy to be worn even by a queen. I wish," Señor Pedrín added wistfully, "that your good father would permit you to remain with me. Doctors are necessary — what would we do without them? But a good bootmaker is precious as diamonds. I will bring the boots to the countess myself. And while I am gone, attend me, Mariano," he said severely. "Remember, perspire!"

No sooner than Señor Pedrín set foot outside the shop, Mariano dropped his work.

"Santiago, you must help me."

"I know nothing of love letters," I protested. "I cannot help you compose one."

"You are the son of the great doctor, are you not?"

"Mariano, you are not listening . . ."

"Besides, I cannot write. I cannot read, either," he said miserably.

"I don't have paper and pencil."

"I will give you paper, all the paper you wish. Oh, Santiago, if you will do this for me, I will teach you to play the guitar. I will teach you to play like an angel."

"I would only play like the devil," I laughed. "Very well. Give me the paper and pencil and I will compose your letter."

I was not sure what one says in such a note. Fortunately, I remembered a number of lines I had read in various books. These I now jumbled together. While I wrote, Mariano regarded me anxiously, fearful that the strain of writing might prove too much for my brain. "Are you all right, Santiago?" he murmured every few seconds.

"Mariano! *Silencio!* How can I think when you distract me?" I closed my eyes, trying to recall exactly what I had read. No wonder Mariano was disturbed; it must have appeared to him that writing a letter is a most painful task!

"There! It is done!"

"What does it say? What have you written?"

"*You* have written, 'Little dove . . .'" I made a face. How foolish such words sounded aloud.

185

"Little dove. *Little dove.* You are a genius, Santiago. Read on."

When the reading was done, Mariano sat back and regarded me with awe. "You should not be a cobbler, Santiago. And you should not be a doctor, no offense to your good papa. You must become a writer. Such language. Such feeling." Mariano put his fingers together, placed them on his lips, kissed them, and then flung his hand upward, the fingers widespread.

"Mariano, we have much work to do."

"You are right. Now let us work." Mariano put the letter, carefully folded, into his pocket, then seized his awl. "We will work twice as fast to make up for the letter-writing time."

That evening I met again with my father in the pigeon house. The lessons continued. *The shoulder girdle is made up of two scapulae and two clavicles. The humerus is attached to the glenoid cavity of the scapula at one end, to the radius and the ulna at the other.* And while I repeated my lesson, I discovered that the bones were beginning to hold much fascination for me. The beauty of line, the conformation of the bones, begged to be drawn. If only I had paper! Paper! Of course!

Next morning, as soon as Mariano and I had a few moments alone together, I asked, "The letter, Mariano? Did she like it?"

He grinned. "Is it not remarkable, Santiago, how a few lines upon a sheet of paper melt the heart of a woman? I think perhaps it is so," he added philosophically, "because words spoken are words lost, but written down, they become eternal. Furthermore," his grin grew wider, "it is something one can show to a friend or two and watch the friend grow sick with envy, is it not? She asks now that I write her another letter, this time in verse. For the son of a doctor, that is no great thing surely, eh, Santiago?" he ended somewhat anxiously.

"In verse? I am not a verse maker. However, I could perhaps be persuaded . . ."

"Tell me what I must do and I will do it. Anything you wish, Santiago."

"Anything?"

"I swear it!"

"I want paper. And pencils. And some charcoal."

"It is forbidden to you! Señor Pedrín has cautioned me. Your father forbids you these things."

I folded my arms. "Then I am sorry. I cannot write another word for you."

"Santiago! I have promised her verses."

"Then write them," I replied coolly. Picking up my awl and a piece of leather, I started to carve out a fresh design I had been thinking of for a new pair of boots.

"You know I cannot write," Mariano said.

I disregarded him.

"Your father would be furious with me."

Silence.

"Señor Pedrín would not permit me to work for him any longer."

Indifference.

"You are a stubborn mule!"

"Love, money, and a good mule are all a man needs

to live well in this world," I replied sunnily. "So Señor Pedrín says."

"The devil take Señor Pedrín, and you with him." Mariano took the awl from my hand. "I will give you the paper . . ."

"And the pencils and the charcoal?"

"And the pencils and the charcoal. But if you are caught, you must promise, on the soul of your mother, that you will not tell who gave them to you."

"I will swear on anything you wish," I said joyfully.

"Tomorrow I will bring them to you," Mariano agreed. "But today you will write the verses for me?"

"At once. Do not talk now. I must think."

I could hardly wait for the next day to arrive. That evening I studied with so much fervor my father was amazed.

"I find it very strange, Santiago," he said slowly, "that your teachers have reported to me that your memory for lessons is so poor. We have done much more difficult work these evenings than you had at school, yet you remember the smallest details. I think perhaps it is not your memory that is at fault; you have been lazy and indifferent."

"No, Papa," I said. "It is not so. I truly cannot remember those things which hold no interest for me. I do not know why my mind rejects such things. I have tried. This is different. I believe it is because I am, as you say, visual. When I can see what the word is, as in these anatomy lessons, my mind grasps and absorbs."

"In that case, you will be happy to hear that

tomorrow night you will help me perform another autopsy. What is more visual than dissection?"

I was dismayed. "Papa! I cannot! I will be sick. My stomach jumps into my mouth at even the suggestion."

"Anatomy is basic to medicine. Books inform, but they do not show you the reality. We will take apart the muscles and glands. We will hold in our hands and examine blood vessels and nerves. You may be sick many times, but eventually your stomach will settle."

"It does not seem right to me," I said miserably, "to cut into the human body . . ."

"Not right?" he flashed. "To the dead one nothing is of consequence, but what you learn from the dead one you contribute tenfold to the living. To be a doctor is to be obligated to life."

I had read in a book somewhere — I do not remember in which book I saw this — that Michelangelo, whose art even my father admired, stole in the dead of night to a chamber wherein lay dead bodies and, choking with nausea and fear, cut into them so that the anatomy of his figures might be accurate. If so great a man found this necessary, surely I could overcome my revulsion.

"I will try to keep my stomach in place, Papa," I said.

Next day I was inattentive to the boot-making; my mind could dwell only on what was yet to come. Mariano was worried.

"Are you not well, Santiago? Perhaps if you were to

step out into the air? Señor Pedrín, I think Santiago is sick. See how pale he is."

"It is true. You are pale . . ."

"Madre de Dios," I groaned. "It is enough to make anyone feel ill . . . he is pale . . . he is this . . . he is that. I ate too quickly this morning. It is nothing. It will pass. See? Already I am feeling better."

When Señor Pedrín's attention was engaged by a customer, Mariano whispered, "I have something for you that will bring health to your cheeks."

"The paper! You have brought me paper!"

From being too pale, I was now fretted over because my face was flushed. I could hardly wait for the day to end. While my fingers dawdled over the leather on the bench, my brain was busily engaged in sketching. Before I had finished the day's work, Señor Pedrín insisted that I go home. When his back was turned, I seized the supplies from Mariano and fled to the pigeon house. I was too excited even to go to the house to eat my supper; I was in a frenzy to get started.

Where does the time go when one sketches? I made drawing upon drawing until all too soon I had used up the paper Mariano had given me. I was so absorbed that I did not even hear my father's footsteps upon the stairs, or notice when he came in behind me. When I realized he was there, it was already too late. My drawings were scattered across the table.

"So," my father said. He reached past me to pick up the papers.

If he destroys my drawings, I thought with anguish, I will die.

TWENTY

THERE ARE SIXTY SECONDS to every minute and sixty minutes to every hour. The hands of the clock move in measured time. Yet is there not an occasion when a minute stretches itself out almost without end, when the hands of the clock falter, and the space between one spoken word and the next is an eternity? So it was now, when I stood in the pigeon house and watched my father reaching for my sketches.

He studied them, one by one, then turned them over and studied them again. I waited. Now, I thought, now my father will rip these sheets down the middle. The frown will gather like the heralding of a storm between his brows; his forehead will furrow; his eyes will grow cold. And his words will be even colder.

Still staring at the sheets of paper, my father said, almost absently, "This is the ischium, is it not?" The ischium, as you know, is one of three bones that form the hip bone. I nodded. "It requires a sharper V-formation," he said critically. "Here." He drew the correct line with his finger.

191

"I can change it, Papa," I said anxiously.

"I know nothing of art," he went on, holding his hand up as if to keep me from interrupting, although I had no desire to speak. "However, I do know anatomy. I am frankly amazed at how much you have learned. You have an instinct for anatomy, Santiago. I think you would do well to make this your chosen field."

"Papa," I said desperately. "Do you never think of anything beyond medicine? What of my drawings?"

"They are well done," he replied with some impatience. "Have I not said so?"

"No, Papa. Not one word."

"If they had been bad or inaccurate, I would have told you so immediately."

This my father considered sufficient praise! He did not know how I hungered to hear . . . what? Enthusiasm? Excitement? A change of heart, even? For him to exclaim, but you are an artist after all! What he did in fact say now, matter-of-factly, was, "Your mother is worried because you have not eaten. Put your papers aside, have your supper, and then we will attend to the autopsy."

The autopsy! I had forgotten. My stomach heaved. The examination of a corpse still lay ahead of me. "If you do not mind, Papa," I said nervously. "I would prefer not to eat."

"In that case, we will save time," my father replied. He went down the steps rapidly. I stood with my head lowered, my mind racing. I had suddenly realized there had been no anger at my disobedience, no question regarding where I had obtained paper and charcoal, not even the threat of punishment. His hand had not for a moment moved toward the whip which lay in the corner where he had flung it after he had discovered the lean-to on Señor Cuideras's roof.

"I am waiting," my father's voice called. I hurried after him.

For one who is not absorbed in the study of medicine, to stand at the dissecting table requires nerves of iron and a stomach lining to match. Several times I felt faint and had to flee outside. Each time I returned, my father, who had opened two books so that I might compare notes between the written page and the actuality, took up his teaching almost from the word where he left off. Even in my agitation, I was able to marvel at his ability. Never, in all the schools I attended, had an instructor been so clear, so patient, so willing to explain over and over again. At one point I became so interested, in spite of myself, that, without thinking, I drew a pencil from my pocket and made a sketch directly in the margin of the anatomy book.

"What have you done?" my father asked.

"Papa," I gasped, "I am sorry. I do not even remember doing this. I will try to clean it off."

"Let it stand." He bit his lips in concentration. "Tomorrow, when we continue our lessons," he said thoughtfully, "I will give you paper and pencils. I believe drawing what you learn will give you a greater insight into what we are doing. Yes. That is what you will do from now on."

I could not believe what I heard. "You will allow

me to draw? You will give me paper and pencils?"

"You are not to waste the paper," he replied sharply. "It is only to be used for anatomical drawings, do you understand, Santiago?"

"I will draw anything you wish," I vowed.

After that, I did not know where the hours went; certainly my father would have worked through the night. Never have I seen anyone who seems to require so little rest, but I am not my father. I do not have his tireless spirit. My eyes began to close. My head drooped. I think I must have drowsed, for I seemed to hear my father's voice as if from a great distance. "It is time to go home, Santiago. I think you are in need of rest."

When we arrived home, my mother met us at the door, her manner agitated.

"It is not right," she said harshly. "He works, works, works, night and day, and there is no time for food. He grows thin and pale. You are a doctor. The son of the cobbler goes without shoes. The son of the doctor goes without care."

"Mama, please. I am fine. Just sleepy."

"Fine! A growing boy who does not eat is not fine."

"It was a matter of his own choosing," my father said. "To miss a meal now and then is of no consequence. And as for working hard, who does not? If Santiago is to become a doctor, there will be many moments of hunger, many moments of weariness. Why does this surprise you? Are you not the wife of a doctor? Go to bed, Santiago. In the morning you will make up for what you did not eat tonight."

194

I staggered up the steps and into my room, hitting against Pedro's bed in the dark. He mumbled, "I am too sleepy for games," rolled over, and filled the room with gentle snores.

"*He* is too sleepy," I muttered. Without undressing, I threw myself across my bed, only for a moment, and woke to find the sun shining and my mother shaking me, insisting that I must come down and have breakfast before I left for Señor Pedrín's shop.

I ate with such appetite that my mother beamed at me. My father was already gone from the house; soon my mother went back into the kitchen. Pedro reached across the table for the bread, from which he tore off a generous hunk, leaving but a small piece for me, and buttering it thickly on both sides.

"What did you and Papa do last night?" he asked. "I did not even hear you come to bed."

"We performed an autopsy."

Pedro put his bread down.

"You know, Pedro . . ." I stuffed a forkful of eggs into my mouth, ". . . it is not too bad when you get used to it."

"Not too bad?" he echoed in disbelief. "To cut up a dead man is not too bad?"

"How else can one truly study anatomy? Are you going to eat your bread, Pedro? I have such a hunger this morning."

"Did it not make you sick? I would be sick." Poor Pedro. He was beginning to turn somewhat green only from hearing about it.

At first I did not wish to admit how many times I

195

had gone out into the night. "I did not feel too happy," I admitted finally, "but it is a remarkable thing, Pedro, to study in the book and then to look down at the body, to examine the muscles, the veins, the bone structure . . ."

"Excuse me," Pedro said hastily and ran out of the room. He had thrown his bread down on the table.

"Santiago," my mother called from the kitchen. "You will be late."

"I'm going. I'm going." I seized the buttered bread and ran off, munching with much appetite as I made my way to the shop of Señor Pedrín.

So the days and nights passed. Once Claudio, Lope, and Francisco waited for me outside the shop.

"You have changed, Santiago," they accused me. "How is it you have no more time for your old friends?"

"What can I do?" I protested. "All day long I make shoes. All evening long I must study with my father."

"You might just as well be back in school," Claudio muttered.

"You were more fun when you were still the wild one," Francisco agreed. "Do you remember how we used to raid the orchards? And the books you read to us on Señor Cuideras's roof? And the time you left us in the woods and got trapped looking into the eagle's nest?"

"Pedro tells us that you are enjoying your anatomy lessons," Lope said sadly.

"Enjoy? Nonsense! Pedro is mistaken. It is simply that I do not have the time," I protested.

"Not even on Sunday?" Claudio asked.

"I will do it," I said. "I will ask Papa to let me join my friends for at least this Sunday. He cannot object after all my hard work. We will meet in the plaza. Agreed?"

"Agreed!" Lope said joyfully. The others crowded around, patting me on the back. "Agreed!" they shouted.

I watched them as they ran off. Pedro should not have said what he did, I thought. It is not true. The idea worried me. Enjoying the anatomy lessons. How could Pedro say such a thing? I started to walk home, then stopped. I have always been honest with myself, if not with others. At least I have tried to be so. Well, Santiago, I asked myself. What are your feelings about this? And I had to answer: the study of anatomy did hold for me a certain fascination and that, in combination with the sketching, gave me a feeling of satisfaction I had not experienced before.

Thus meditating, I finally arrived home and found that a visitor had preceded me some little while before. I had not seen him since my father had brought me home from Huesca.

"Don Carlos!" I was so glad to see him I almost threw my arms around him. He shook hands with me gravely, although his smile was warm.

"How are you, Santiago? You are well?"

"I am well, thank you. Papa," I cried, "Don Carlos wrote to you, do you remember . . ."

"I remember well." The cold note was back in Papa's voice.

197

"I promised myself that I would speak to you in person, Don Justo."

"You have spoken eloquently," my father said drily.

Don Carlos rose from his seat. "I have brought you a gift, Santiago, which, with your father's permission, I should like to give you now." He went to a table and picked up a package wrapped somewhat carelessly. Before I accepted it, I glanced at my father. He nodded. I tore off the wrapping; the paper fell heedlessly to the floor, and I stood there, rooted to the ground, when I saw what Don Carlos had brought me.

"Water colors!" I said unbelievingly. Real water colors, not colors manufactured tediously from cigarette papers, but such as a true artist uses. I could not look up, for tears were stinging my lids.

"You have not thanked Don Carlos," my mother said, coming in at that moment to ask us to gather round the supper table.

"He has thanked me, Señora," Don Carlos said quietly, watching my lowered face.

"Please, Mama, if I may be excused," I begged.

"What? You wish to miss your supper again? It is becoming impossible," my mother said, her voice beginning to rise with agitation.

"You are excused," my father said in a tone that settled the matter finally. My mother subsided unhappily. I did not wish to bruise her feelings, but I was seized by such excitement that, had I eaten, I would have choked on the food. Clutching my gift, I hastened to the pigeon house.

What to paint! What to paint! What to paint! It

was an agonizing decision. My mind flew in all directions. I would paint saints. No, I would fill the paper with ships at sea, I who had never seen a ship, never felt the salt spray of the ocean upon my face. A bullfight! I was in a fever. But in the end, and why I did this I do not know, I made a delicate anatomical sketch, and then another. Long after I was finished I stayed on in the pigeon house, staring out the window across the roof of Señor Cuideras's roof. When the shadows of night touched down upon the earth, stealing softly in through the window, enfolding me in darkness, I stirred. Gathering my sketches, I made my way slowly back to the house.

The supper dishes had been cleared away. Don Carlos was tapping his pipe clean against his hand. My father was listening intently. The talk was of politics: how the times we live in are disturbing, the people are restless with new ideas and desires, the spirit of revolution hangs over us all, the queen cannot long endure.

"Ah, Santiago! I see you have already used the water colors," Don Carlos said, smiling. "May I see your work?" I handed him the sheets mutely, for I was still in that curious withdrawn mood that had enveloped me in the pigeon house.

"Excellent!" Don Carlos said after a long pause, but he sounded puzzled. "But surely your choice of subject is somewhat . . ." he hesitated, ". . . surprising?"

My father took the drawings from Don Carlos. He regarded them silently, without expression. Then he said, "Not surprising in the least, Don Carlos. Santiago has developed into a fine student of anatomy. It was a natural choice for him to make. May I offer you a cigar, Don Carlos? Another glass of wine?"

My drawings were put to the side. The men resumed their conversation of generalities. I felt close to tears. These special moments I had lived in the pigeon house, were they so meaningless? My sadness brought me to the point almost of desperation. Look at me! Look at me! I wanted to shout. Do you not see Santiago Ramón y Cajal, artist? It was fruitless. I was sure they did not even see me leave the room. I climbed the steps like an old man, despondent and weary.

Pedro was already in bed, with a guilty look upon his face. When I entered, he said, "Oh, it is only you, Santiago." He pulled a book from beneath his pillow. "I know we are forbidden to read such books," he sighed, "but I have forgottne what happens to Robinson Crusoe. I will let you read it when I am finished, if you wish."

"I've already read it," I said shortly. "Do you not recall that I read it to you last summer?"

"Yes. But I do not have your memory for stories, Santiago. Besides, it is such a wonderful book."

We heard steps upon the stairs. Pedro slammed the book shut and thrust it under his pillow again, falling back with his eyes closed, pretending sleep.

The door opened; Papa stood silhouetted in the doorway.

"May I come in?" he asked politely. He did not wait for an answer, but entered. He leaned against the window as he talked. "I have done much thinking regarding your future, Santiago. And yours, too, Pedro. It is not necessary to keep your eyes closed when you are wide-awake, Pedro. Now attend me, both of you."

Pedro sat up, looking somewhat abashed.

"I have this day received notice that I have been given an appointment as a professor of dissection in Zaragoza."

"But that is magnificent, Papa," Pedro shouted.

My father continued as if Pedro had not spoken. "Before the summer is over, we will be moving there. There is an old dissecting room no longer used in the garden adjoining the hospital of Santa Engracia. There we will continue our lessons in anatomy, Santiago. And you will begin to attend also, Pedro. And you will both attend school in Zaragoza."

"So my fate is sealed, Papa? And Pedro's? We are both to study medicine? This is your final decision?" I asked unhappily.

He looked surprised. "But this has always been my decision," he replied. "However, I have also come to another decision. When you register for school, you may also register for classes in art."

My father moved away from the window at last. As he went out the door, he said quietly, "Pedro, if you wish to read in bed, either keep the book in plain sight or hide it better. It is jutting out from under your pillow." He closed the door but immediately opened it again.

"I have looked at your water color paintings again,

Santiago. Paint for me a portfolio of such water colors, and I will have them made into a book. Go to sleep now. You must be up early in the morning."

I could not speak! I could only stare at Pedro, who was grinning at me from ear to ear.

Epilogue

Eduardo visited me again this morning. He is a crafty fellow, this Eduardo. He comes as a friend, but it is the doctor who looks at me and scolds, "Don Santiago. You must rest."

"Eduardo," I reply, "I am eighty-one years of age. I am dying. No. Do not interrupt. I am," I say with good humor, "enough of a doctor to be able to diagnose my own disease."

He turns his head away and grief overwhelms him. Poor Eduardo. How we doctors battle to wrest life from the grip of death; how bitter we find it when we must lose.

"Eduardo," I tell him sternly, speaking to him as former teacher to former pupil. "I forbid you to be sad."

He smiles. "You are right, Don Santiago. Let us talk of new honors you have received."

"What? Do you think this is a daily occurrence?" I ask with mock severity. He nods.

"Frankly, yes. I do not know any man who has received as many honors as you. Such titles! Such prizes! Such decorations! A monument for you in the Parque del Retiro . . ."

"A place for birds to perch," I interrupt. "When I am gone, Eduardo, people will pass by that monument without seeing it. And if one stops, he will say, puzzled, 'And who, *por favor,* was Santiago Ramón y Cajal?' "

"And what of the institute?" Eduardo asks, indignant that I am making fun. He speaks of the *Instituto Cajal,* which is being built on the hill of San Blas and which will house not only my own Laboratory of Biological Research, which I headed for over twenty years, but other laboratories as well. Yes. I am pleased. I am flattered. But this is not so important to me as other things, not nearly so important as my work. "In the world of science," Eduardo continues, "you are a giant. And you will be remembered as a giant."

I sink back against my pillow, and immediately he is alarmed. "What is it?" he cries. "You are in pain?"

"I am merely following the orders of my doctor and resting. Shall I tell you something, Eduardo? At one time, I wanted nothing so much as to become an artist."

"An artist? But what a loss to science!" he exclaims.

How strange the direction one's life takes. I remember how enthusiastic my father was when I first began to make anatomical paintings in water colors. He was even going to make a book of them for me. But in those years, it was not possible to make proper reproductions of these paintings. And so this dream

204

was never realized. My father kept his word about my classes, however. He permitted me to take as many art courses as I wished. How soul-satisfying they were! But never did he lose sight of his objective. For three years after we moved to Zaragoza he made me work with him in that small, shabby dissecting room. If I close my eyes, I can see that room more clearly than the one I am in now; I can hear my father's voice. "Always, Santiago, always remember the human body is an extraordinary piece of machinery, delicate, intricate, magnificent. You must come to know it as a fine musician knows his instrument." My father was tireless. He demanded much of me, but always he was prepared to give as much of himself.

"Do you know, Eduardo," I say, "that I was a poor student?"

Immediately Eduardo springs to my defense. "You must not say such things about yourself," he reproaches me.

"Why not, if I tell you the truth? My father worried. A position was available as director of anatomical museums in the faculty of medicine in Zaragoza, for which I applied. It was doubtful if I would get it. My father was most pessimistic. 'If you do not get this appointment, then you must become a doctor in some small village, perhaps even return to Ayerbe,' he told me. But I was most fortunate. I did in fact become director. How much rested upon that one appointment, Eduardo! It was at that time I chose to enter the field of microscopic investigation."

Eduardo stood up. "You are growing too weary,

Don Santiago. I insist that you rest now." He picked up some papers which had fallen from my bed. "And you are not to do any more writing for the moment. I forbid it. If you do not listen, I shall have to take the papers away."

"I will obey," I say meekly.

I did, indeed, doze for a while, which is not strange, considering my age and my weakness. Soon, however, I shall pick up my pencil and write again. I have written many scientific books and papers. And I have also put down on paper my ideas about life and love and nature, thoughts on any subject! The story of my life I began for my eldest son. How sad that he died long before I finished it.

In spite of Eduardo and the others who hover about me, I shall go on writing and working until the hand of death reaches out and stills my heart. You see? I have not changed. I am still as stubborn as María Ruíz's mule.